THE KEY TO
TAROT

THE KEY TO TAROT

FROM SUITS TO SYMBOLISM
ADVICE AND EXERCISES
TO UNLOCK
YOUR MYSTICAL POTENTIAL

SARAH BARTLETT

FAIR WINDS

Inspiring | Educating | Creating | Entertaining

Brimming with creative inspiration, how-to projects, and useful information to enrich your everyday life, Quarto Knows is a favorite destination for those pursuing their interests and passions. Visit our site and dig deeper with our books into your area of interest: Quarto Creates, Quarto Cooks, Quarto Homes, Quarto Lives, Quarto Drives, Quarto Explores, Quarto Gifts, or Quarto Kids.

First published in the United States of America in 2015 by Fair Winds Press,
an imprint of The Quarto Group,
100 Cummings Center, Suite 265-D,
Beverly, MA 01915, USA.
T (978) 282-9590 F (978) 283-2742
www.QuartoKnows.com

Fair Winds Press titles are also available at discount for retail, wholesale, promotional, and bulk purchase. For details, contact the Special Sales Manager by email at specialsales@quarto.com or by mail at The Quarto Group, Attn: Special Sales Manager, 401 Second Avenue North, Suite 310, Minneapolis, MN 55401, USA.

ISBN: 978-1-59233-813-9

Digital edition published in 2015
eISBN: 978-1-62788-761-8

Conceived, designed and produced by
Quid Publishing
Part of The Quarto Group
Level 4 Sheridan House
Hove BN3 1DD
England

Design and layout by Clare Barber
Illustrations by Joanna Kerr

Printed in USA

TO ALL THOSE WHO HAVE FOLLOWED THE FOOL'S
MAGIC PATHWAY

CONTENTS

INTRODUCTION

There is something innate in all of us called "curiosity." This curiosity leads us to follow pathways, to nose around in our own and other people's lives, and sometimes to take an unknown route when we are supposed to follow a known one. Curiosity often leads us astray. Curiosity is also about delving into the past and the future. We are curious to know what will be—either because we seek guidance when making choices, or sometimes to avoid responsibility for our choices.

Many times I've heard people wail, "I'm fated, the fortune-teller told me!" The tarot has become a curiosity, in part due to its power to reveal future energies or outcomes, but also thanks to its symbolic nature, which many dismiss and others embrace. The tarot is, like any other divination tool, a connection at the very moment of time you consult it, between you and the Universe. But this is not "fate," as we will discover later.

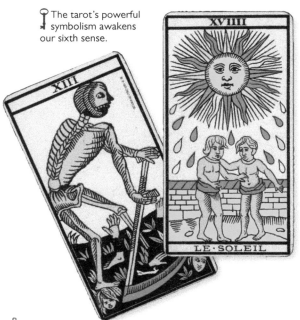

The tarot's powerful symbolism awakens our sixth sense.

I first became curious about the tarot in my early twenties when I went to a village fete and the vicar's wife, draped in velvet scarves, bangles clinking around her arms, took on the role of fortune-teller. She had a deck of cards, the Marseille deck if I remember, and I thought, I want to know my future! The reading was like many others, at a time when the tarot was still considered a gypsy scam: "You will meet a tall dark stranger, but you must avoid him. The blonde man who comes into your life will be with you forever." Warnings and judgmental statements are not part of the tarot, they are part of the people who read the tarot! Of course, we take heed, we listen, we absorb the fortune-teller's words unconsciously, and we often twist the words to fit our life story depending on our perception of what we want to happen.

A few weeks after the village fete, a chance encounter with a friend led me to Paris, where I fell in love with a tall, dark stranger, an artist and poet. In fact, he seemed like the perfect man for me, and he gave me a beautiful deck of tarot cards and taught me all he knew about the tarot. I spent six months living the life of a bohemian artist with him in a garret on the Rue de Rivoli. Although we had to part, my tarot journey really began then, like the Fool setting off to discover more. Not stepping off the edge of the cliff, but stepping across the ravine to another pathway, where all would become clear. The tall dark stranger was actually a gift, not someone to be avoided. It was then that I wanted to know more and to find out why the vicar's wife had read the cards the way she did.

Fortune-telling is really a means to understanding the decisions you make.

This book is about the keys you will need to get through the doorways of knowledge, skill, and self-awareness to lead you on your own true tarot path. We are all Fools, all curious, but some of us are ready to find out more than others. With *The Key to Tarot*, you can access the truth about yourself and others and also get in touch with your mystical connection to the Universe.

The best way to use the tarot is to read it, not to guess or make judgments like the vicar's wife. Enjoy unlocking the keys to your own tarot journey, and be true to your own mystical potential.

CHAPTER ONE

THE KEY
to the
BASICS

- ⊶ The tarot is a mystical pathway to hidden knowledge

- ⊶ Sacred numbers connect us to cosmic energy

- ⊶ Learn how to care for and use your cards

- ⊶ Understand card positions and the focus card

A BRIEF HISTORY OF THE TAROT

The tarot is usually made up of a deck of seventy-eight cards, although some early decks have a different number. Each card has a name, number, and specific image, which work together to create the card's meaning. The tarot is quite simply a universal language spoken through the use of archetypal symbols.

THE ORIGINS OF TAROT

No one is really sure of the true origin of the tarot, but for the last three hundred years or so, occultists, writers, and historians have all had a good shot at proving its source, colored by their own personal view of the tarot. But most believe that the tarot originated several thousand years BCE in ancient Egypt, when places such as Giza and Abydos were centers for mystical practice and the worship of gods. Certain symbols were created to produce a secret language only known to initiates of these mysteries, and these were probably inscribed onto tablets, and later written onto scrolls.

Tarot cards first appeared in Europe in the fourteenth century, and they were used throughout the courts of Europe, by nobles and ladies, both as a card game and as a fortune-telling device. It was believed that the deck arose from a combination of early Italian playing cards and the set of twenty-two mystical cards which had appeared in esoteric circles of Europe and filtered into the hands of kings and courts.

This fifteenth-century "joker" may be the predecessor of the Page court card in later tarot decks.

The beautiful renaissance Italian Visconti-Sforza deck was one of the earliest to include 22 mystical cards, such as the Star depicted here.

In the same century, the tarot was also used to play a game known as "tarocchi," later known as "Trumps." The earliest decks were all exquisitely hand painted, and with the Renaissance's revival in ancient esoteric mysteries, tarot decks, such as the Visconti-Sforza deck, painted for the fifteenth-century duke of Milan, began to appear.

THE MEANING OF "TAROT"

Antoine Court de Gébelin, an eighteenth-century French linguist and freemason, believed the word "tarot" was derived from the name of the Egyptian god of wisdom, Thoth. He went on to suggest that the twenty-two main cards were based on an ancient set of tablets of mystical wisdom, saved from the ruins of a burning temple. This "Book of Thoth" outlined a secret language in which all gods could be contacted through hieroglyphs and numbers.

He also discovered that the hieroglyph "tar" meant "way" or "road," and "ro" or "ros" meant "king"—put together this means the "royal road of life." From stone carvings, there is evidence that sets of Thoth tablets were used by pharaohs to discover their future.

Thoth, the Egyptian god of wisdom and magic, revealed divine knowledge to priests.

Gébelin was convinced the tablets or early scrolls were brought into Europe by traveling magi. He later went on to develop his own tarot deck using seventy-seven cards, plus the Fool, to make seventy-eight. The Major Arcana contained three times seven cards, plus the Fool, and each of the four suits of the Minor Arcana contained twice seven cards. This became the foundation of most tarot decks today. It encapsulated the mystical nature of the number seven.

Some nineteenth-century scholars prefer to believe the word "tarot" is partly formed from an anagram of the Latin word rota, meaning a wheel. In occult circles, rota means the eternal ending and beginning of cycles of change, as revealed through tarot card readings. French Kabbalist and philosopher Eliphas Levi (1810–1875) believed the tarot was rooted in the sacred Hebrew alphabet, also associated with mystical numbers. By the end of the nineteenth century, the British occultist Dr. Arthur Edward Waite (1857–1942) and American artist Pamela Colman Smith had developed their own deck. Waite was an initiate and one of the founders of the esoteric group known as the "Hermetic Order of the Golden

The vivid imagery of the Rider-Waite deck tells your story.

Dawn," which also included Edvard Munch, Bram Stoker, and William Butler Yeats. The Rider-Waite deck, as it is known, has become one of the best loved and most used decks due to its highly pictorial imagery. The Universal Tarot deck, used throughout this book, is based on the Rider-Waite deck.

In the 1940s, British occultist Aleister Crowley also designed his own deck, known as the Thoth deck. Crowley believed the tarot was an intelligence in itself, and a key to the archetypal world within each of us. His ideas led to the later development of the tarot as a tool for unlocking not only your mystical talent, but also your archetypal and psychological potential.

The powerful depiction of Death from Crowley's Thoth deck.

CONNECTING TO THE MYSTICAL NUMBER SEVEN

1. Take your tarot deck and place seven random cards laid out facedown on a table in a straight horizontal line.

2. Close your eyes and run your fingers back and forth along the line of cards. When you feel the moment is right—in other words, you sense or think it's time to stop moving—touch one of the cards.

3. Open your eyes, turn over the card, and look at it. Don't attempt to project any interpretation onto it, just study the image, its number, its words. Although this is the first card you chose, it is also the most mystical because it is this first moment of pure random choice that connects you to the universal energy via the seventh harmonic, the mystical vibration of the cosmos. Remember, the mystical number seven is not necessarily about the seventh card drawn in a layout or spread—it is the first card we choose, the most meaningful and insightful in any layout. We'll find out later how to interpret this.

CHOOSING YOUR DECK

With so many decks to choose from, you may wonder how you can possibly find one that you truly like, or one to which you find an immediate connection. If you're a complete beginner, start with the Universal Tarot deck used throughout this book, or the Rider-Waite deck, which is similar. The main reason is that both include imagery for the numbered cards. Learning to read the numbered cards without a pictorial "clue" can create confusion until you've mastered the art of reading.

Here are some other decks that you might like to use later, once you are used to the different imagery and have a greater understanding of the numbered cards, the court cards, and the suits. The Major Arcana (the twenty-two main pictorial cards) are usually fairly similar throughout most decks, so it's these images to which you'll be attracted first.

THE TAROT OF MARSEILLES

This is probably the most well-used deck of all, and it was the first tarot I came across when I began my journey in Paris many moons ago. The deck first originated in France in the sixteenth century, and its powerful, simple images evoke emotions and feelings deep within. Although simple, it is still striking and effective. There are no pictures for the Minor Arcana, so it can be difficult for beginners to interpret.

THE GILDED TAROT

Designed by Ciro Marchetti, this is a superb deck, rich in classic imagery. It keeps to the traditional use of court cards with King, Queen, Page, and Knight. Its illustrations are a mélange of modern machines and medieval robes, but it works superbly.

The Tower card from the Tarot of Marseilles, probably the most well-used deck of all.

THE NEW MYTHIC TAROT DECK

This deck by Juliet Sharman Burke and Liz Greene, with illustrations by Giovanni Caselli, has simple imagery and is often recommended for beginners. The bonus is that all the pip, or numbered, cards are also individually illustrated, and the symbols are clear and easy to understand.

AFFIRMATION FOR ACCEPTING YOUR CHOICE

Once you have chosen your deck and it is finally in your hands, this is the first time you will connect to the pack, so it's important to affirm your acceptance of its powers.

1. Prepare your room by lighting some incense and a candle to create a calm and mystical atmosphere. Sandalwood incense enhances psychic power; pine or rosemary bring clarity and focus.

2. Place five white quartz crystals (or rose quartz if you prefer) in a circle (big enough to surround your deck of cards) on a table.

3. Take the cards from their packaging and place them in the center of the circle.

4. For one minute, close your eyes and relax so that you are in harmony with the tarot energies. Now say the following affirmation:

My choice is done, my word is true,
This tarot pack is good and new.
With mystic power and secret sight
This deck will bring unworldly light.

5. Blow out the candle and the incense and gather your pack together. Keep it in a silk scarf or special box when not using it to protect its psychic powers.

CARING FOR YOUR DECK

Once you have chosen your deck, now is the time to understand that it has a life of its own! This deck of sacred knowledge, in whatever form or style you choose, is a pathway, like any other, with difficult terrain to cross, mountains to traverse and beautiful scenery to take in. It is as real as the natural world around you.

We need to put trust, care, energy, and love into the things that take us nearer to our own inner truth or guiding voice, so caring for your deck is as important as caring for your child, friend, lover, parent, or self.

Although tarot is a symbolic pathway, it is also a vehicle for mystical revelation, connecting you to the energy of the Universe through its symbols. So by analogy, the tarot can be thought of as not only the route the tram takes, but the tram itself that carries the travellers. If you care about the way you make your mystical journey and the vehicle that takes you down that route, this ritual will ensure that the deck of cards (both the journey and the vehicle) are made sacred for your personal use.

Most tarot readers protect their deck, either by putting them in a special box or tying them up in silk or other natural fabric, or by placing them somewhere special such as on an altar or sacred corner of a room. Whether you already have a deck of tarot cards stashed away in your drawer, or have just acquired a new one, you must cleanse the deck of any negative energy it may have accumulated on its way to your table.

 Protect your tarot deck by placing it in a drawstring bag made of natural fabric.

CLEANSING THE DECK

Follow this exercise ritual to make sure your cards are protected and blessed. You will need five white candles—to invoke the powers of the five tarot spirits—and your deck of tarot cards.

1. Take the cards and lay them in a stack before you on a table.

2. Now take the five candles and place them in a pentagram shape (a five-pointed star with the first point at the top—see illustration) around the table, leaving enough room to spread the cards out in a random swirl with your hands.

3. The first candle represents the spirit of the Major Arcana; the second the spirit of the suit of Swords; the third the suit of Wands; the fourth the suit of Pentacles, and the fifth the suit of Cups.

4. Randomly spread out all the cards in front of you, in a shuffling motion around and around on the table.

5. Next, light the candles, close your eyes, relax and just for a moment calm your mind by counting down slowly from ten to one, then repeat the following (either aloud or in your head) five times to reinforce your deck's power:

> *By the light of the First, Second, Third, Fourth and Fifth*
> *This deck is blessed with sacred love*
> *By night or day, its power I'm given*
> *To bring me all I need from above.*

6. Now, gently open your eyes, run your hands across all the cards and then stack them back into a deck. Now place the cards in their special place.

This ritual will clear all negativity from the deck, and bring you closer to its power as a tool for self-understanding and future predictions.

THE DECK'S STRUCTURE

A standard deck of tarot cards is made up of twenty-two main cards, known as the Major Arcana, and four suits of fourteen cards, called the Minor Arcana, making seventy-eight cards in total. Arcana is the Latin plural of arcanum, meaning "secret." So the Major and Minor Arcana mean "big secrets" and "little secrets."

The Major Arcana represents universal archetypes—qualities or experiences that are common to us all, such as happiness, sadness, truth, belief, desire, jealousy, anger, love, and hate. An archetype is a quality, essence, blueprint, or an original model of behavior, personality, feeling, experience, or idea. Throughout history, certain words, symbols, or codes have been used to describe these archetypes.

And it is through symbols that we recall the ancient archetypes that are common to humankind. According to the psychoanalyst Carl Jung, we all resonate with these symbols because they are carried in both our personal and collective unconscious.

The Minor Arcana generally represents the way these qualities or archetypes manifest in daily life. For example, the court cards represent people who may influence you in some way according to the suit and the qualities they represent (see pp. 92–93 for more about what they represent).

These four suits, or "tarot spirits," combine with the spirit of the Major Arcana to make up the powerful symbol of the pentagram, which represents the oneness of the Universe (see illustration). This is a useful symbol to work with as it signifies your own inner connectedness to that mystical place.

The tarot is made up of the Major and Minor Arcana.

EMPOWERMENT RITUAL

Perform this little ritual to enhance your understanding of the structure of the deck and to empower you with the energy of Fire, Earth, Air, Water, and the fifth energy—that of the Universe.

1. Light a white candle, place it on your table, relax, and close your eyes for a few seconds to calm your mind. Take your tarot cards and randomly mix them all up, facedown, on the table; swirl them round and round in circles for at least a minute until they are thoroughly mixed up. Then draw them into a pile and place the stack face up in front of you.

2. Now comes the hard work! From your stack, first remove all the Major Arcana cards and place in a separate stack in the middle of your table. Also remove and gather together all the four different suit cards into their own piles. Place the four stacks of suit cards at each of the four directions as follows:

```
              PENTACLES


   CUPS      MAJOR        SWORDS
             ARCANA


              WANDS
```

Wands to the south of the Major Arcana cards (i.e. below the deck); Swords to the east of the Major Arcana (to the right); Pentacles to the north (or above), and Cups to the west or to the left.

Wands and south = Fire
Swords and east = Air
Pentacles and north = Earth
Cups and west = Water
Major Arcana at center = Universe

By handling all the cards in this way, you are becoming more in tune with the different energies and structure of the deck. Say the following affirmation to keep you in touch with this empowering energy every time you work with the tarot:

I trust in my tarot guides of
Fire, Earth, Air, Water,
and the Universe
to bring me the results and destiny
I choose whenever I work with them.

UNDERSTANDING SYMBOLS

T he word "symbol" is rooted in an ancient Greek word, symballein, which means "throwing together." A symbol, then, or this "throwing together," is literally the merger of the divine realm and the manifest world. In other words, a symbol allows us to cross the bridge between the known and the unknown, and across which the seeker of truth can travel too. Carl Jung wrote that a symbol is "something more and other than itself, which eludes our present knowledge." This is also, in Jungian psychological terms, when the deep realms of the unconscious are momentarily connected to the conscious, resulting in our experience of "meaning."

Symbols are universal motifs appearing throughout civilizations, which give "meaning" to human existence. Since the dawn of humankind, we have had an innate urge to express core human experiences such as childhood, virility, fertility, death, sacrifice, or love, through art, myths, dreams or belief systems. Wherever in the world a civilization or culture has been, and whatever the time period, symbols are a universal language transcending all.

If you think about it, the tarot is exactly that, a combination of symbols, both numerical and pictorial, which connects us to timeless myths and collective dreams.

In our daily lives, we often wander around without even noticing these universal symbols and how they affect us. For example, we may see a red rose, we like the smell or color; we do not consciously think, oh, it's a symbol of love and red is a symbol of passion. Or when we eat strawberries, do we realize they were once a symbol of chastity?

Yet symbols take us into the unknown depths of ourselves. So take time to look closely at the images on every card, as well as the significance of the numbers and the associations with astrological energy and themes. We read the tarot as if it were a language, but it takes time to get to know it well. The language of symbols is rich and carries many layers of meaning, but most importantly, this language can tell you all about yourself.

ASSOCIATIONS

To understand the many-layered language symbols, take for example the image of a rainbow (see illustration). Throughout different cultures, the rainbow has been a symbol of light, a bridge, or a messenger from the divine. But what does a rainbow "say" to you? What do you associate it with?

1. Close your eyes now and visualize your own rainbow. Is it as brilliantly colored as the one on the picture, or more? When you see a rainbow in the sky, what do you associate it with? Pots of gold, light, the rain, a divine presence, or nothing?

 For example, in Hindu belief, the rainbow is the thunder god Indra's bow, while in the traditional Shinto belt ancestral spirits used to descend to Earth. In Tantric Buddhism, the seven colors of the rainbow, which make up the clarity of pure light, represent the penultimate meditational state before attaining enlightenment. In ancient Greece, Iris, the rainbow goddess, was a messenger of the gods.

2. Throughout the day, look for other common symbols around you. When you realize you live in a symbolic world, then tarot reading suddenly becomes a deeply enriching and life-changing experience.

USING THE CARDS

When you first start using the cards, there are various practical steps to take into consideration. As you get to know the deck, you will also start to use your own rituals for shuffling and drawing cards, but here are some of the most basic and well-known methods to get you started.

SHUFFLING

There are probably as many ways to shuffle as there are cards! Tarot cards are larger and thicker than normal playing cards, and with seventy-eight, shuffling isn't all that easy. If you have reasonably long fingers you can try the old card method of dropping half from one hand through the other half in the other hand. Some people just spread them out facedown on a table and swirl them around.

An important part of shuffling is that while you are doing it, you should also be thinking deeply about what you are asking the tarot or the Universe to reveal to you. So, it's not just a question of mixing the cards up, it is a question of making them as random as possible, enabling you to connect to the universal well of knowledge.

Shuffling the cards brings you in direct contact with their invisible energy.

ASKING THE RIGHT QUESTIONS

Before you even start drawing or choosing cards, you need to know what kind of questions to ask. For example, will you get the job you interviewed for? Or, you might wonder if a lover is thinking of you. Alternatively, you may have a choice to make between going abroad for a great opportunity or staying where you are and not leaving family and friends. The first query isn't difficult to ask. Repeat your question over and over in your head as you shuffle the cards: "Will I get the job?" For a question this simple, which requires a basic yes or no answer, or even a "don't know yet," you would only require one card to give you an answer, or maybe two at most. For the question regarding the lover, there are various spreads you can use to find out (see the chapter on spreads), and again this isn't a difficult question to answer.

It is the last query about making a choice that is the most difficult to reply to. If you phrase a question as a "shall I or shan't I" you can't expect the Universe to make a subjective human judgment. So it's all about phrasing. Therefore, you would be better off asking two questions. The first: "If I opt to go abroad, is this a good time?" The second, "If I stay at home, will I be happy?" That way you can make a decision based on the two outcomes.

KEYNOTE

Try this simple shuffling method:

- Split the deck into two.

- Take one half and swirl it around on the table for a few moments, then draw the cards together into a pile. Now do the same thing with the other half of the deck. Finally, put the two stacks together to make one, and cut the cards a few times.

DRAWING THE CARDS

There are many ways to randomly choose the tarot cards, but here are my two favorites:

FIRST METHOD:

1. After you have shuffled the deck, place the deck facedown and then slide the cards gradually to the right (or left) with your hand until you have made a long line of overlapping cards.

2. As you do so, constantly think of your question, if you have one.

3. When ready, slowly run your finger along the line of cards until you feel a card that is "asking to be picked." I often prefer to close my eyes when doing this.

4. Continue doing this until you have the right number of cards for your spread. As you draw each card, place it face up and upright in its numbered position as described in the spreads in Chapter Four.

SECOND METHOD:

1. Shuffle the cards as usual, then take the deck in one hand facedown or away from you. With the other hand, fan the deck out until most of the cards are visible and overlapping.

2. Close your eyes and run your finger across the fan; when you feel the moment is right, pull the card from the deck and place it face up on the table. This is a much harder way of drawing cards, but it is very useful if you don't have a lot of space, or you are doing a reading for a friend. Your friend can then draw cards from your hand, rather than you both making a big tarot mess on the table.

PLACE AND TIME

Tarot readings are best done in a quiet place, with soft lighting, candles, or incense to set the scene and to create a genuinely calm atmosphere around you. Focus clearly on your questions if asking specific queries, and don't try to do too many readings in one day about the same issues; this will only lead to confusion.

OPEN READINGS

Apart from using the tarot for asking questions, you can also use it to give you a general sense of what's occurring in your life right now. This is known as an "open reading," where you don't ask a question at all. For example, you may be at a crossroads with work and need some direction, or obsessed about a relationship when in fact you need to be developing your personal talents.

Once you learn how to interpret cards, open readings can give you valuable information about yourself and your needs. In Chapter Four, there are some practice spreads to give you deeper insights into yourself.

OPENING UP TO THE UNIVERSAL ENERGY

The following exercise will give you a sense of opening yourself up to the universal energy.

1. Shuffle the cards and don't think of anything in particular. Just try and stay calm, relaxed, and have an open mind. Close your eyes if this helps. Shuffle for about two minutes. Then place the stack on the table, and open your eyes.

2. Cut the cards randomly, and look at the card that is revealed as you turn up the top half of the deck. This card will tell you all about "you now." You can turn directly to the card interpretations in Chapters Two and Three to give you a brief keyword to sum up you right now. Check your response to the card's interpretation—do you agree? Are you doubtful? Do you feel a connection to the card?

MIRROR, MIRROR

The tarot can be used as a tool to help you to make crucial decisions, to confirm your true desires for the future, and to enhance your self-understanding. This extraordinary deck of cards is a mirror of opportunity and a reflection of the Universe at any one moment.

When you are gazing at a tarot card, you are not only gazing at yourself, but into the waters of the Universe, which, like ripples on a pond, reflect back the light of mystical truth. By using the tarot, you will discover more about the "you" that you see in the mirror. But perhaps more importantly, you will discover how you are at one with the Universe, as is the deck of cards you are about to use.

THE WELL OF KNOWLEDGE

This exercise will help you to understand that the universal well of knowledge is open to us all. Just by looking at the images, you are already connecting to the energy of the Universe and seeing the truth of that moment. You don't need any prior knowledge of the tarot.

1. Without shuffling, simply take any card from the deck and place it facedown on a table in front of you. Put the rest of the pack to one side.

2. Breathe slowly and relax for thirty seconds, then turn over the card and gaze at the image. The image is irrelevant. Even if you have picked a seemingly unattractive card, like the Tower, realize that you're simply taking one glimpse inside the universal well of knowledge, available to anyone who looks at the cards. The difference is, you're going to learn how to tap into this universal energy to reveal the truth about the past, present, and future, for yourself, and perhaps later, for others.

3. Say aloud what the card depicts. Be as objective as you can. For example, if it is the Fool, you might say: *"A young man walking toward the edge of a cliff without looking where he's going."* Or you might say: *"A foolish rogue about to leap across a mountain in search of happiness."* It all depends on you how you interpret this card. This is the key link to the energy of any moment and to the power of using the tarot as a mirror of truth.

LETTING GO OF WHAT YOU WANT TO SEE

As human beings we don't have much choice but to color our view of the world with our character traits and personal experiences. So it's inevitable that you're going to "project" emotions, feelings, and desires onto the cards and onto your interpretation.

We all do this as we look at the tarot cards, consciously or unconsciously. But if we try at least to be aware that we are doing it, and maintain an objective distance, then we're halfway to understanding what the tarot is all about. Oneself. Be very, very honest with yourself when asking questions and when giving yourself answers.

We all want to get positive cards to affirm what we believe is right or want to happen. But the tarot is not about good or bad, these are simply values we place on certain words and images. For example, consider the word "change" as represented by the Death card.

The Death card can spook some people, simply because they don't understand its true meaning.

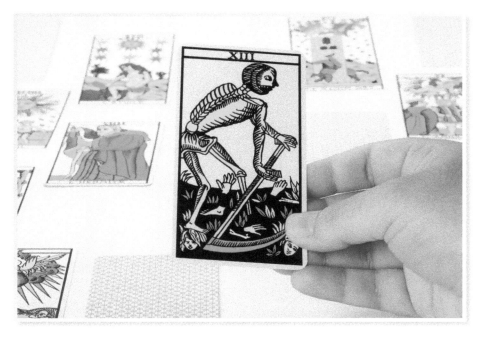

Do you fear change? Do you avoid it, or do you welcome it? Take the Death card from the pack and study it. Does it alarm you? If so, now is the time to embrace the card and know that something can be changed in your life to make it vivid, positive, and creative. The tarot enables you to confirm your gut instinct or intuition, so in a way it is simply mirroring your intuitive powers too.

Letting go of what you want to see or happen is the hardest part of tarot reading. Use the interpretations I've given in the main part of the book to guide you and you will soon be able to interpret from a mixture of traditional meaning and personal involvement and intuition. The only thing you can be sure of is that the tarot never lies, only people do, and that you might not see all there is to see. Trust your intuition, not your projected values.

ACCESSING YOUR INTUITION

Here are some practices to get in touch with your intuitive or sixth sense. Try this for a few days as you go about your daily business. Use your imagination and trust in it because it is part of your intuitive mind.

1. When you're driving around in circles looking for a parking space, imagine one in your mind, see a space empty, or a car just pulling out leaving you with the space. Really believe in that space and it will appear!

2. Walk down a street and imagine just before you turn a corner, a stranger you are about to walk past. Describe to yourself, or visualize in your mind, their shape, height, weight, face, eye color, and so on. Turn the corner, and you may be surprised by your intuitive moment.

3. Practice using your intuition by following your hunches or gut instincts about situations rather than following logic or reason. For example, you're driving to work and have a sudden feeling that there's going to be an almighty traffic jam, so trust in that hunch and take another route. Follow your intuition, don't ignore it.

The more you practice working with gut feelings, the easier it will be to be intuitive about the tarot, which means you can also start to take control of your life.

CARD FOR THE DAY

Now that you've got to know a bit about the background and usage of the tarot, here's a ritual to perform every day to get to know the cards more intimately. As you develop your skills, and become more aware of your mystical connection, you will find you develop your own rituals and pre-reading warm-ups. But this will get you off to a good start.

Each day, take a different card. In other words, if you draw the same card two days running, replace it in the pack and choose another. This is about "understanding" the mirroring influence of each card, not part of interpreting a card. The cards you choose will have different effects on you. Some will be likeable and easily understood, while others may be mysterious, complicated, or provocative in some way. Be aware of your reactions to the cards rather than trying to interpret them.

Our reaction to a card's imagery also tells us how we view the world at that moment in time.

PICKING YOUR CARD
FOR THE DAY

Here's how to choose a card for the day, and how you can get to know each card better as the day progresses.

1. Shuffle and relax as normal, and then cut the deck three times.

2. Now randomly draw a card from the deck; you don't have to fan it out nor spread it on the table. Just simply run your finger along the top of the cards until something "speaks" to you. Then cut the pack at the place chosen and look at the card.

3. Write down the name of the card and your reaction to it.

4. Finally, leave the card in a safe place while you go about your daily business, but during the day make notes or observations of how the card might be mirroring you and the day.

When you first start working with a card for the day, you'll also see how uncannily the card corresponds to the energy, experiences and events throughout the following twenty-four hours.

THE HIGH PRIESTESS

The High Priestess: A day when secrets may be revealed, or a female mentor will be of benefit to you.

The Star: Opportunities abound, and creative contacts will give you fresh ideas.

THE STAR

CARD POSITIONS

Throughout the interpretations on the following pages, I focus on three main positions used in the spreads. The "you now" card is the first card you lay down, and often the most crucial to any reading. The "blockage" card is usually (when included) the second card placed horizontally across the first card, and the "outcome" card is the last card drawn; this can sometimes be used as an interpretation for one of the "future" cards too.

EXAMPLE SPREAD

1. You now
2. Blockage
3. Past
4. Future
5. Outcome

THE FOCUS CARD

When you do a reading, whether with three cards or ten, you will find that the "you now" card usually colors or flavors all the other cards in the layout. It's a bit like putting a load of pale clothes in the washing machine with a red dress—the red will permeate the other fabrics, turning them a little pink. Similarly, there are certain cards that become "focal points" in a reading. The focus card will be explained in more detail in Chapter Four.

REVERSED CARDS

Reversed cards (i.e. when you draw a card and the picture is upside down facing you) cause a lot of controversy among experienced tarot writers and readers. Most tarot readers who do use reversed cards believe they imply the quality or energy of that card is somehow lacking or not available to the reading, and others believe the reversed card is the opposite of the upright interpretation. The latter, although harder to interpret, does enrich the whole reading process. However, it is not something you need to learn yet. As a beginner, turn the cards to the upright position, and they'll reveal as much as you need to know for now.

🔑 You don't need to worry about reversed cards as a beginner, just turn them the right way round.

CHAPTER TWO

THE KEY
to the
MAJOR
ARCANA

- ⚷ The Major Arcana is a journey of self-discovery
- ⚷ The cards are mirrors of your soul
- ⚷ Direct experience of the card energy from the exercises
- ⚷ Interpret the cards in relation to the issue or question

GETTING TO KNOW THE MAJOR ARCANA

The Major Arcana is a potent symbolic language, representing the archetypal qualities or fundamental energies and experiences in life. But this "secret" wisdom is no longer so cryptic if you start to connect to these qualities and understand why you react to some cards with fear, mistrust, passion, or no feelings whatsoever. This is simply because you are looking at a mirror of yourself, and the cards to which you most strongly react are reflective of your current needs, desires, and issues. The ones you hardly glance at may be issues in your life you have denied, repressed, or simply never realized were in need of attention.

THE FOOL

THE MAGICIAN

THE HIGH PRIESTESS

THE EMPRESS

THE EMPEROR

THE HIEROPHANT

THE LOVERS

THE CHARIOT

STRENGTH

THE HERMIT

THE WHEEL

JUSTICE

DISCOVERING THE MAJOR ARCANA

1. Separate the Major Arcana from the rest of the deck and spread them face up across the table or floor so they are all visible and placed in five horizontal lines of four cards and the last line with two cards. Place them in numerical order as in the illustration, with the Fool as zero placed first, followed by the Magician and so on. Now you can begin to see how these cards are stepping stones on your own personal journey.

2. Move your finger from card to card as you look carefully at all the images, reflect and observe your reactions. If any card gives you the shivers or you feel an affinity, make a note on a piece of paper, and look up the brief interpretation to see what qualities you are resonating with.

3. Finally, look at all the images at once. If any one card stands out, look up its interpretation. It may be a potent card in your life right now; perhaps the Universe is telling you to attend to these issues.

THE HANGED MAN

DEATH

TEMPERANCE

THE DEVIL

THE TOWER

THE STARS

THE MOON

THE SUN

JUDGMENT

THE WORLD

WORKING WITH EACH CARD

E ach of the Major Arcana has a story to tell, either corresponding to an archetypal motif as recounted in ancient myths, or aligned to your own life journey. But to really engage with the mystic nature of the tarot, we need to experience these stories too. So I have devised a series of exercises, including visualization techniques, magic spells, spiritual or meditational affirmations, and creative work, to take you into the world of tarot archetypes. To experience the tarot is the only true way to understand the invisible, universal energy, which permeates all things and unites everything.

If you follow the tarot journey in the chronological order set out in the following pages, by actually engaging in the energy of the card, you will learn how this is not only a mirror of your own self but of the infinite part of yourself that is connected to the Universe.

Each card also has a section on general meanings and interpretations, and it gives basic interpretations to guide you when placed in the main positions used within spreads. This mustn't be the only way you interpret the cards, though; the intuitive part of reading the tarot will come to you without you even realizing it, so by the time you've worked through this book you will have unlocked the first doorway to your own potential.

This is then followed by an exercise or creative practice to enable you to experience the power of each card.

FATE AND FREE WILL

Some of us think we are fated, and that the cards simply tell us that fate. But before we explore each card individually, it's useful to understand that fate and free will are not mutually exclusive. "Fate" may seem to be something that happens without conscious intention, and "free will" something that happens through personal choice. But making choices and also meeting the unexpected are both part of the deeper resonance of "you" in the Universe. Because they are both part of every moment, the two energies are simultaneously in play when using the tarot. Do not think "I am fated," think more, "my character is my fate."

MAKING SOMETHING HAPPEN

The tarot wakes up a part of ourselves that we aren't consciously aware of so that we can consciously act upon that knowledge and "make something happen."

1. To understand the above paradox better, choose any card randomly from the Major Arcana cards.

2. Place it face up on the table, look up the traditional interpretation if you need to, and now say in your head or aloud "what kind of choice can I make?" In other words, I am not going to feel fated. I am going to take responsibility for my choices even if they are inspired by seemingly random influences.

So with the tarot, fate and free will are one. When you choose a card, it digs deep into your psyche to awaken you to consciously do something about this card, or wake up this mirrored bit of yourself, and make SOMETHING happen. This is the secret power of the tarot—it actually brings unconscious knowledge to conscious awareness, so you can live your life the way you truly want to.

ASTROLOGICAL AFFINITIES AND NUMBERS

Here is a simple chart to show you how each of the cards is linked to an astrological sign or planet. Although these affinities vary according to certain tarot decks and writers, these are the most commonly used. These simple keywords are the beginning of building up a picture of what the cards mean, like stringing letters together to make a word.

As in the old esoteric formula, "as above, so below," the mirror doesn't just work reflecting the tarot to you and back, but on into infinity, mirroring the very essence of the archetype. These "essences"—described as "forms" by Plato—were once believed to be harnessed via the planetary powers, which are simply mirrors themselves of the archetypal web of the Universe.

MAJOR ARCANA CARD

- The Fool
- The Magician
- The High Priestess
- The Empress
- The Emperor
- The Hierophant
- The Lovers
- The Chariot
- Strength
- The Hermit
- The Wheel of Fortune
- Justice
- The Hanged Man
- Death
- Temperance
- The Devil
- The Tower
- The Star
- The Moon
- The Sun
- Judgment
- The World

ARCANUM NUMBER	ASTROLOGICAL AFFINITY
0—Unlimited potential	Uranus—Freedom
1—Focused action	Mercury—Magic
2—Mystery	The moon—Receptivity
3—Abundance	Venus—Indulgence
4—Authority	Aries—Organization
5—Knowledge	Taurus—Respect
6—Love	Gemini—Choice
7—Self-belief	Sagittarius—Achievement
8—Courage	Leo—Power
9—Discretion	Virgo—Discrimination
10—Destiny	Jupiter—Opportunity
11—Fairness	Libra—Compromise
12—Paradox	Neptune—Transition
13—Change	Scorpio—Transformation
14—Moderation	Cancer—Cooperation
15—Temptation	Capricorn—Materialism
16—The Unexpected	Mars—Disruption
17—Realization	Aquarius—Inspiration
18—Illusion	Pisces—Vulnerability
19—Joy	The sun—Vitality
20—Liberation	Pluto—Rebirth
21—Wholeness	Saturn—Accomplishment

Now you are ready to set forth on your tarot journey and experience the Major Arcana and the archetypal nature of life, so you can truly engage and understand every card.

THE FOOL

KEYS

- ⭘─ Adventure
- ⭘─ Spontaneity
- ⭘─ Impulse
- ⭘─ Infatuated
- ⭘─ Blind to the truth
- ⭘─ Eternal optimist
- ⭘─ Ready for romance, a quest, or a risk

THE FOOL

MEANING

The Fool seems to be heading to the edge of a cliff without looking where he's going. A dog yaps at his feet but, careless and carefree, the Fool looks only to the distant mountains, his mind only on his quest. But the Fool is smarter than you might think. In fact, isn't it possible that he is very aware of his path, and is just about to cross to another ledge a pace away, and continue his journey? Only he knows the answer. Similarly, when you draw this card, it reminds you that sometimes taking a risk is far less "foolish" than it seems.

EXAMPLE INTERPRETATIONS

The Fool often turns up in relationship questions and signifies that you may be infatuated or blind to the truth. However, it can also mean that the romance is flourishing and taking a risk in love isn't such a bad idea. In the "you now" position, interpret it as "I'm falling in love fast; this is an adventure, and I'm ready for romance." Or you're ready to take a leap of faith. In the blockage position, the Fool signifies that your irresponsible attitude is preventing you from moving on. In the outcome position, you're about to go on a journey of self-discovery or find romance.

PACKING YOUR FOOL'S BAG

Taking the first step of the Fool's tarot journey is a bit of an adventure too. It's like a first romance or infatuation because you're not sure where you're going and what to expect. But like the Fool, your journey is going to be fun if you develop your trust in the cards as your personal guides.

WHAT YOU WILL NEED:
• A piece of paper, pen, and imagination
• A white quartz crystal

WHAT YOU WILL EXPERIENCE:
• A sense of excitement and wonder as you begin your journey

1. Imagine you have a bag or backpack just like the Fool, or a bag that you could carry easily on a long journey. Now draw it on the piece of paper, or copy the Fool's bag from the illustration. Write your name on the bag.

2. Now think about what you would take with you on your journey. You can take five different items (there are five tarot spirit energies). These five things can be anything you like: practical items you'd need on a journey, things you can't be without, ideas or concepts, in fact anything that you think matters to you or you love dearly. Take your time, don't rush—once they are written on the paper, you can't change them.

3. Write down the five items beneath your bag.

4. You are now about to set off on a journey—it can be anywhere you like, as long as there is a destination in your mind. Write down the name of the place or destination at the bottom of the paper.

5. Finally, fold up the paper and put it in a secret box or drawer. Place the white quartz crystal on top to charge it with illuminating energy, and remember you are investing your own spirit of adventure into this tarot journey—it will bring you to a deeper connection to the Universe. You're not going to look at the paper again until the end of your tarot journey.

THE MAGICIAN

KEYS

- Getting magical results
- Acting with awareness
- Persuasion
- Time to manifest
- Concentration brings results
- Knowledge is power
- Channeling power

THE MAGICIAN

MEANING

With the mysterious infinity symbol above his head, the Magician is the archetypal miracle worker. He reaches up to the heavens to invoke the powers of the planets, and with the other hand points to the tangible world, where his work can manifest. He has a wand, a cup, a sword, and a pentacle on his table—a sign of his complete knowledge and oneness with the Universe, corresponding to the alchemical blend of mind, body, spirit, and soul.

EXAMPLE INTERPRETATIONS

When you draw this card, you have the ability to merge imaginative ideas with practical solutions to bring you creative results. It's also time to play with ideas and find the best way to get what you want. The Magician also signifies that as long as you are aware of your own motivations for doing what you do, you will succeed.

In the "you now" position, you're in balance with the Universe, and you can harness its powers to help you achieve your best. In the blockage position, only "you" matter, which prevents useful influences helping you out. In the outcome position, you will soon be inspired to get the results you are seeking.

HEAVEN AND EARTH SPELL

This exercise will give you an experience of the power of the Magician, and how you too, if you truly believe, can invoke the power of the Universe to help manifest your dreams.

WHAT YOU WILL NEED:
- Five white quartz crystals
- Five white candles
- A piece of paper and pen

WHAT YOU WILL EXPERIENCE:
- A feeling of being a miracle worker

1. Place on a table the five crystals in the shape of a pentagram—as shown in the diagram—with the fifth point of the star at the top. Beside each crystal, place a candle, then light the candles. These magic ingredients symbolize the four elements Earth, Air, Fire, and Water and the spirit of the Universe, which will protect you while you perform this spell.

2. Now draw a horizontal figure of eight (the infinity symbol) on the paper, and place it in front of the pentagram of crystals and candles.

3. Close your eyes for a few seconds to relax and to get in tune with the mystical energy, then repeat the following spell:

> By the power of the Earth
> I will bring thoughts to fruition
> By the power of Air
> I will speak and be heard
> By the power of Fire
> I know what I desire
> By the power of Water
> I will give back to the Universe
> what I have taken
> By the power of the Universe
> I will manifest my dream.

4. Blow out the candles, and as you do so, you will feel the Magician inside you coming to life, ready to work your own personal magic.

THE HIGH PRIESTESS

KEYS

- Secrets
- Silent potential
- Feminine power
- Intuition
- Mystical influence
- Seeing the truth

THE HIGH PRIESTESS

MEANING

Ruled by the moon, the High Priestess knows the inner world of emotions and identifies with her mystical connection to the Universe. She represents the archetype of the "unknown becoming known," and the link between awareness and our unconscious. With lunar symbols at her feet and the crown of the Triple Goddess on her head, the High Priestess often appears in a reading when a secret is about to be revealed to the querent. Behind her hangs a veil of embroidered pomegranates, symbolic of the veil of illusion that life is. Working with this card can help you to see beyond the obvious and tangible to what is hidden and true.

EXAMPLE INTERPRETATIONS

When you draw the High Priestess in the "you now" position, it often signifies that you are holding back a secret, or have feelings or desires that you don't want to be known. It is also a sign that it's time to trust your inner voice or intuition. In the blockage position, you are finding it hard to express your feelings to yourself or someone else, or fear what you truly feel about someone. As an outcome or future card, someone else is going to reveal a secret to you, or you may be enlightened as to why something hasn't worked out as you wanted it to.

THE MOON AND THE VEIL

This simple exercise will bring you closer to your own inner High Priestess. Do this exercise in the evening after nightfall, when you are alone and relaxed.

WHAT YOU WILL NEED:
- Three moonstones (or three white crystals of your choice)
- A small veil of fine silk tulle or organza
- A blue or purple candle (representing lunar light)

WHAT YOU WILL EXPERIENCE:
- The serenity of the High Priestess and your hidden psychic potential

1. Take the three moonstones and place them in a triangle on a table or floor, to invoke the power of the Triple Goddess in her guise as the High Priestess.

2. Place the blue candle in the middle and light it. Now repeat the following affirmation as you gaze into the candle flame:

> *I welcome the hidden side of myself,*
> *my own High Priestess,*
> *who like the Triple Goddess reveals*
> *all knowledge and truth.*

3. Next, move the candle to one side, and place the veil over the three moonstones. Now say out loud or whisper one secret that you would never tell anyone; repeat it three times. As you speak, gaze at the veil and beyond it to the moonstones.

4. How do you feel having revealed your secret? Elated? Shocked? Relieved? Guilty? Whatever it is, feel it, because feeling is the experience that will bring you closer to your own inner High Priestess who knows all secrets.

5. Now take the veil away from the moonstones and say this affirmation:

> *My hidden potential is there*
> *before me.*
> *I only have to look.*

THE EMPRESS

KEYS

- Sensuality
- Pleasure
- Self-indulgence
- Mothering others
- Feeling good about life
- Creativity

III

THE EMPRESS

MEANING

We all take pleasure in the earthly delights of the world and the Empress is the female expression of that joy. Whether through touch, music, art, sex, nature, or eating a box of chocolates, we all love to indulge ourselves. Yet the goddess Venus, who rules this card, is not just about motherly love and earthly pleasure. She is also about vanity, wily deeds, and envious actions. When you draw this card, you may immediately take it to mean generosity or motherly love, but it can also imply a literally interfering mother, or that you are smothering someone with too much love. However, as an abstract influence, the Empress reveals that you need to stay grounded, and you can be assured of progress in any plan.

EXAMPLE INTERPRETATIONS

In the "you now" position, this card means you may be strongly identified with the Mother Earth archetype. You have all the qualities of the Empress in your favor—take care that you are not exaggerating them. How you go about using them will be determined by the rest of the layout. If drawn as a blockage card, a disruptive female is stopping you from moving forward; as an outcome or future card, your creativity is about to be of huge benefit.

MIRROR, MIRROR
ON THE WALL

This simple spell will put you in touch with your own inner beauty, creative power, and sense of self-love.

WHAT YOU WILL NEED:
- Mirror
- Candle
- The Empress card

WHAT YOU WILL EXPERIENCE:
- A sense of feeling like Venus, vain yet bountiful and fair

1. In the evening, place your candle on a shelf, table, or ledge in front of a mirror. Light the candle to the left of the mirror, and prop the Empress card against the mirror on the right.

2. Relax and focus first on the candle flame for about two minutes to still your mind. Then turn your attention to the mirror, and look yourself in the eye. Imagine you are Venus, beautiful, dazzling, the most lavish of all the goddesses. As you continue to stare at yourself, repeat the following enchantment:

Mirror, mirror on the wall
I am the fairest of them all
Of all who love, I love the best
Of all who give, I give the rest
Of all who take, I take the least
Of all dark pleasure, I am the feast.

3. Now look at the image of the Empress, and take the card in your hand. As you gaze at it remember the card is a mirror, just like the one before you. Now you are mirrored twice—by looking at the glass and by looking at the card. Look from your reflection in the mirror to the reflection of you on the card. They are one and the same.

4. Next, make an affirmation:

Thank you, Empress,
for showing
that the beauty in me is both
for others and for myself.

5. Finally, blow out the candle and feel empowered by your own inner Empress.

THE EMPEROR

KEYS

- ⚬— Authority
- ⚬— Leadership
- ⚬— Organization
- ⚬— Control
- ⚬— Assertive and structured

IV

THE EMPEROR

MEANING

Corresponding to the astrological sign of Aries, the Emperor balances the lavish indulgences of the Empress with order and structure. As the archetypal "father figure," the Emperor also embodies the masculine principle of leadership. With his long white beard, he appears to be as wise and as old as the mountains behind him. His throne is embellished with ram heads—the motif for Aries and the sense of accomplishment and organization. This card often suggests that official matters need attention, or that there is some older, wiser, father figure type coming into your life who can advise you. In a relationship issue, you may be about to fall for a father figure.

EXAMPLE INTERPRETATIONS

As an outcome card, you may be about to meet an authority figure, who can sort out any professional or financial matters in your life. Alternatively, the Emperor may arrive in your life in the guise of a lover or friend. It can also mean you are attracted to a dominating person but can't free yourself from their control or power. As a blockage card, someone in power is hindering your progress, and as a "you now" card, it's time to become a father figure for yourself—take action, be assertive, and start to face the facts.

HAVE A DECLUTTER

To really understand the power of the Emperor, you are now going to prove to yourself how organized you can be.

WHAT YOU WILL NEED:

- An untidy room, home, cupboard, or an outdoor area that needs tidying
- A sense of humor
- Your tarot deck

WHAT YOU WILL EXPERIENCE:

- Being a truly organized individual like the Emperor

1. Look at the room or place you're about to tidy up. How long have you been putting this job off? Has there been a time when you faced it, smiled, and said to yourself, "I am going to do it now," and then didn't? Well, you're going to do it now.

2. Remove everything from the cupboard or mess, then make three different piles: things you need, things you like or want, and things you don't need or want. Make sure you are keeping things that you truly need or want. Once you have sorted your things, be as ruthless as the Emperor could be and go through the "wanted" items again, and try to remove at least three things that are "not truly important."

3. Now replace everything that you are keeping and get rid of the rest (whether to recycle, to give to charity or to put in the trash).

4. Now take your deck of tarot cards, and remove three cards randomly. Set them out in a line on a table and look up their meanings if you're not sure of them yet. Could you do without these in your life? What qualities do they represent? The "Emperor" in you can now decide whether you want to keep these qualities or declutter them from your character. It's up to you to decide, but like the Emperor, with organization and discipline, you can not only clean up your home, but clean up your act too.

THE HIEROPHANT

KEYS

- Respect
- Spiritual teacher/guru/mentor
- Establishment
- Religious heritage
- Doing what's expected of you
- Conforming to a group
- Using traditional methods
- Discovering belief

MEANING

If the Magician invokes the power of the Universe to manifest dreams, then the Hierophant takes traditional or religious ideas to achieve results. In other words, the card often represents the traditional leader or mentor of any society or belief and respects its laws. The crossed keys symbolize the keys to the conscious and unconscious realms. Two initiates kneel before our friendly mentor, ready to take a leap of faith or a rite of passage. When you draw this card it can indicate that you're about to meet someone who will influence you in this way, or that you will have to do what is expected of you if you are to arrive at a chosen goal.

EXAMPLE INTERPRETATIONS

In the "you now" position, the Hierophant reveals you may be stuck in your ways and are not yet ready to change or move forward, or that you are relying on conventional opinions and have not yet developed your own. In the blockage position, you may be fighting against a restrictive influence such as a dogmatic partner or friend. It could be that you need to liberate yourself from family assumptions. In the future or outcome positions, you are going to meet a guru, adviser, or teacher who must be trusted and can lead you to better self-understanding.

THE HIEROPHANT WITHIN

This exercise is designed to give you utter self-belief—a belief based on knowing that you are a guru yourself.

WHAT YOU WILL NEED:
• Lots of scraps or pieces of paper
• A pen

WHAT YOU WILL EXPERIENCE:
• Understanding the Hierophant in you

1. Use as beginnings of sentences the examples given below to help you write down (each on a scrap of paper) what makes you feel confident, alive, motivated, and sure of yourself. For example, you may feel exuberant when you ride a bike, fearful when you're performing in front of an audience, and so on. Write as little or as much as you like for each category.

My current aim in life is…
I feel most confident when…
I truly believe in/that…
My greatest knowledge is about…
I love learning about…
I have a passion for…

What I fear most of all is…
My self-esteem is low when…
I don't believe in…
I know nothing about…
I don't want to learn about…
I hate…

2. Think about your reactions and feelings when you write these all down. Now put them aside, and then look at them again a few hours later. Remember, these are all symbols of you, the Hierophant. Now you're going to conquer the negative feelings by crumpling up the bits of paper with the negative words written on them and throwing them in the trash. Take the positive sentences as the guru in you coming out to teach the world of your discovery in the nicest possible way. Repeat them as affirmations every day.

THE LOVERS

KEYS

- ⊶ Choices in love
- ⊶ Romance
- ⊶ Temptation
- ⊶ Commitment
- ⊶ Power of love
- ⊶ Physical attraction
- ⊶ Love triangle
- ⊶ What love means to you

VI

THE LOVERS

MEANING

The Lovers card has many associations and sometimes as tarot readers, we can get confused as to its real meaning. This card is not just about "happily ever after love"—it's about "choices" in love relationships. These choices encompass a range of experiences such as who we choose to fancy, adore, be with, encounter, desire, obsess about, hate, and so on. The card asks you to reflect on what love is, including your reason for asking a love question.

EXAMPLE INTERPRETATIONS

Are the naked lovers about to merge or to part? Angels are messengers, so what message is this angel bringing to the couple? Is it to bless them as they make a vow or commitment, or a warning of the price of infidelity? Is there some kind of love triangle going on? A serpent coils around the Tree of Forbidden Fruit. Serpents are symbolic of sexual desire and betrayal. Is this choice about being tempted to do wrong, or a choice to free oneself from temptation when a commitment is to be made? The answer all depends on what you project onto the card and the circumstances surrounding your question. The best way to deal with this card is to interpret it first as "love choices must be made," before reading the card in relation to others in a spread.

MY STORY OF THE LOVERS

Everyone experiences love in one way or another, but what does it really feel like to you? This exercise will help you to understand the Lovers card's meaning, but more importantly, what your relationship to love is all about.

WHAT YOU WILL NEED:

• A tarot journal
• A pen
• Two pink candles

WHAT YOU WILL EXPERIENCE:

• Knowing what love means to you

1. Light the pink candles to invoke a romantic atmosphere, and place the Lovers card on the table in front of the candles.

2. As you focus on the card, reflect on what love means to you. Write down whatever comes into your mind in your journal, headed: "My story of the Lovers." Freely associate words and phrases with this card without any self-reproach or judgment, or write a story around what you see. The words can be as vivid, lurid, sexual, careless, and carefree as you want.

The whole point of working with the Lovers is to keep the romantic ideal of perfect love in your mind, but open yourself to other possibilities (i.e. that love can also be blind; love hurts; love is not always forever, and so on). Again, if you "truly love someone," what does that mean? Or, how do you deal with the guilt or passion of a secret love affair on a daily basis? You will find that as you get close to understanding both positive and negative aspects of this card, you will begin to see your own emotional investment in the card's complex language. This is why journal work is essential to keep a record of your changing views and feelings during the course of your developing intuitive process.

THE CHARIOT

KEYS

- ○—ᴛ Willpower
- ○—ᴛ Achievement
- ○—ᴛ Control over feelings
- ○—ᴛ Learning to keep on track
- ○—ᴛ Trusting in the self
- ○—ᴛ Being determined
- ○—ᴛ Wanting victory

VII

THE CHARIOT

MEANING

The Charioteer is ready for action. As the archetypal self-starter, he knows he is going to get ahead, and conquer new lands. The Charioteer is dressed in armor, fearless of battle, and accompanied by two sphinxes that represent the balance of light and dark, masculine and feminine, power and submission. In fact, our hero is fearless and carries with him the Magician's wand to signify he believes he has the power of the Universe on his side, as he struts forth under a canopy of stars. When you draw this card, it indicates you will overcome all the odds with your vitality, focus, and sense of direction.

EXAMPLE INTERPRETATIONS

In the "you now" position, you are motivated and convinced you will succeed. This is a great time to join in the competition and win. Your confident nature will bring you rewards, and if you assert yourself, success will be yours. As a blockage card, you have a mission, but you haven't quite committed yourself to the direction you're going in. It is time to take the chance and get on with it. As an outcome card, asserting yourself and staying on top of a situation will mean you will gain great success.

STANDING TALL MEDITATION

To really get in touch with the archetypal achiever, you must learn to walk tall and be as courageous as he/she is.

WHAT YOU WILL NEED:
• You, barefoot and wearing light-fitting clothes

WHAT YOU WILL EXPERIENCE:
• Knowing you can conquer the world

1. Find a quiet place alone. Stand up straight with your feet almost close together. Close your eyes and concentrate your mind on the soles of your feet. "Snuggle" your bare feet into the floor beneath you. Feel the weight of your body spread evenly through you, then imagine yourself rooted to the floor by strong, tree-like roots.

2. Next, bring your mind into the base of your spine, and feel the center of yourself aligned and growing tall. Lift your chest up and away from the abdomen, hold your buttocks in, and lengthen your spine up towards the crown of your head. Soften your shoulders, lengthen the back of your neck, and bring your attention to the uprightness of your spine. Be aware of the vertical strength of yourself and then walk forwards. Take one slow step, and each time you move forward imagine your goal is that step, and the achievement being all yours. You have now walked tall with the Charioteer.

STRENGTH

KEYS
- Gentle force
- Inner strength
- Personal power
- Compassion
- Tolerance
- Taking responsibility
- Overcoming obstacles

VIII

STRENGTH

MEANING
If the Charioteer's bravery is fearless in the face of battle, the lady taming the lion knows that inner strength is needed to conquer the senses, desires, weaknesses, or ignorance. This kind of strength comes from spiritual and psychological acceptance of oneself and others. With love and patience, you can change things that on the surface may appear threatening or unstable. The lion represents not only a wild animal but also the wildness in oneself. This card is often a sign that we have come to terms with our inner misfit and can take responsibility for our lives.

EXAMPLE INTERPRETATIONS
When Strength appears in the "you now" position, it usually indicates you need to gently force an issue to achieve results. You are resilient and in control of your life, but you must also face others who may need careful handling. In the blockage position, Strength asks you whether your kind heart and tolerant attitude is allowing others to walk all over you. Perhaps you need to develop some emotional boundaries? In the future or outcome position, good persuasion and a little compassion will get you results. In love questions, it often indicates that you are giving too much and not getting anything back in return.

CHAKRA STRENGTH

To enhance your own inner strength, this exercise helps to balance the chakras, the invisible energy that circulates through and around your body, connecting your physical body to your spiritual self. In the accompanying illustration, the seven main chakra energies are indicated with a color for each. As you strengthen your chakras, visualize the corresponding color fill the relevant chakra with its colored light.

WHAT YOU WILL NEED:
• Comfortable, light-fitting clothes

WHAT YOU WILL EXPERIENCE:
• A sense of inner strength and compassion towards yourself

1. Find a quiet place alone, and sit cross-legged on the floor if you can. If not, just sit on a chair. Close your eyes and first visualize the color red at the base of your spine, the chakra known as the "base" chakra. Imagine it firmly rooting you to the floor or chair.

2. Hold your hands about 7.5cm (approximately three inches) away from your body over the pubic bone area. Have the fingers of each hand pointing at each other, almost touching. Gently and slowly move them upwards to the sacral chakra, just below your navel. Each time you reach a chakra, imagine the color associated with that chakra—strengthening, toning, and filling you with spiritual light. Do the same with the other chakras as you move your hands up to the final crown chakra, and the color violet.

3. Now place your hands back in your lap, and visualize closing down the chakras as if you were closing doors in a hallway. Start with the crown chakra and work down, imagine the color then the door closing on the color. This way you have strengthened and protected the inner you. Strength will be yours.

THE HERMIT

KEYS

- Discretion
- Withdrawal
- Looking for direction
- Wanting solitude
- Soul-searching
- Detachment
- Looking for meaning in life
- Inner contemplation

THE HERMIT

MEANING

There are times when we need to withdraw from the world and think about ourselves, our goals, our needs, and desires. What is life really about? What does it all mean? The archetypal Hermit in you does exactly this. When he is activated we contemplate, reflect, do some soul-searching, or just hide away for a while. When you draw this card, it's time to step back and ask yourself what you truly want. In fact, it may be that you need to change your whole life direction, rethink your future, or find a new purpose in life. It's as if your soul or your inner voice is demanding to be heard. It can be a lot of fun, seeing that there are other ways to live your life.

EXAMPLE INTERPRETATIONS

In the "you now" position, think long and hard before you make any decision, and don't be impulsive about any long-term plans. You need to take a step back, maybe even three steps back, before you can move on. If this is a relationship issue, you may need to be alone for a while to see objectively where you're going. As a future or outcome card, you may have to wait a while before you know which direction or goal is the right one for you. As a blockage card, your resistance to other people's advice or hesitant attitude is holding you back.

THE SOUL ALONE

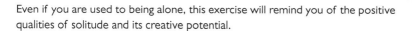

Solitude can be highly creative, yet some of us resist being alone for fear of our own thoughts. This exercise will show you that you are never alone when you are part of the Universe.

WHAT YOU WILL NEED:
- A bag or pouch containing ten crystals or stones
- A real flight of stairs, or at least ten steps you can walk down

WHAT YOU WILL EXPERIENCE:
- The power of being at one with yourself

Even if you are used to being alone, this exercise will remind you of the positive qualities of solitude and its creative potential.

1. Sit somewhere peaceful and alone, close your eyes and imagine yourself walking down a flight of stairs to an empty basement. It is filled with beautiful light, color, and a welcoming angel-like figure who is your soul's companion. Here, you chat together and contemplate what and where you are going next. After your visit, you climb back up the stairs to the world, refreshed, and creative about your life.

2. Next, take your ten crystals and head to a real staircase or flight of steps. Start at the top of the stairs and walk down slowly. On each step, stop and take one crystal from the bag and place it on the step, until there are ten crystals on ten steps.

3. If you haven't reached the bottom of the staircase, continue on down until you do. At the bottom, repeat the following spell:

With crystal power and Hermit love
Wisdom comes, white as a dove
This soul alone will see the answer
A time for truth for ever after.

Now go back up the stairs and collect each crystal on the way, place in your pouch and keep in a safe place to remind you that you're not a lonely soul but a magical one.

THE WHEEL OF FORTUNE

KEYS

- Destiny
- Timing
- Each moment is a new beginning
- A turning point
- Inevitability
- Repeating cycles
- "What goes around, comes around"

X

THE WHEEL

MEANING

The Wheel's message is that if you don't join in the cosmic dance, you may get left behind. This card embodies both fate and free will. It implies that the Universe is in constant movement, the wheel forever turning. Even though you may feel a victim of outside forces (fate), remember that in every obstacle or crisis, there is opportunity; so don't sit around weeping about your lot—get up and engage in life. Even if you don't get to go where you intend on going, it may be that you have to go down another road first to see the possibilities. It's also about accepting things—good and bad—when they turn up, and working positively to adapt, make choices, and know things will improve.

EXAMPLE INTERPRETATIONS

In the "you now" position, this is a card of new beginnings. The timing is right, so go with the flow; it's time to jump on the bandwagon and take the chances coming your way. As a future or outcome card, unexpected events will provide a turning point in your life, so don't hold back or resist. As a blockage card, your feeling of being fated is stopping you from making important decisions. This card always implies a pivotal time to adjust your outlook accordingly.

CREATE YOUR OWN FORTUNE

If we truly believe we can change our lives for the better we will, but most of us need some kind of "luck" too. This exercise will help you write your own positive fortune.

WHAT YOU WILL NEED:
- Paper
- A pen
- The Wheel of Fortune card

WHAT YOU WILL EXPERIENCE:
- Being part of the Wheel of Fortune

1. On your piece of paper, draw a wheel with twelve spokes, just like the one in the diagram. Between each spoke, write one wish so you have twelve in total. They can be anything as long as they are realistic enough to come true. So, for example, if you wish you were a millionaire, that's actually attainable if you are clever enough, but to wish you had wings may not be.

2. Once you have completed your wish list, take the Wheel card and place it on top of your own wheel to empower it with universal energy. Close your eyes, and say the following affirmation:

Whatever changes or opportunities the Universe brings me, I know that deep within me I am part of the cosmic dance, and the Wheel will show me the way.

It may well be that one of your wishes comes true.

JUSTICE

KEYS

- Fairness
- Harmony
- Justice
- Objective attitude
- Accepting responsibility
- Making decisions

XI

JUSTICE

MEANING

Justice simply implies that some kind of judgment is being made or will be made. The archetypal "lady of the scales" is associated with the sign of Libra, ruled by the planet and goddess Venus. Of course, Venus wasn't at all "fair" and was renowned for being seductive and manipulative. So when you draw this card, take care that you are being as objective as possible about making decisions, or that you are not judging yourself or others from a personal point of view. On another level, this card can also mean that law suits or legal issues are current keys to the querent's future happiness.

EXAMPLE INTERPRETATIONS

In the "you now" position, you are more rational than usual and can make good decisions based on logic and reason. However, if this is in a blockage position, it could be that you're either being too compromising or, like Venus, your sense of fairness is tainted by manipulative tactics! As a future card, take care that you are absolutely non-judgmental in all dealings; it can also mean that legal issues are about to be resolved in your life. As an outcome card, you will have to account for your actions or take responsibility for your decisions. If you do so, success will be yours.

LEARNING TO BE A GOOD JUDGE

Good judges are impartial. They attempt to avoid any emotional investment in a situation. As we are all human beings with feelings and hidden agendas, this isn't exactly easy. This exercise will bring you closer to an understanding that labeling something "good" or "bad" depends on your perspective of the world.

WHAT YOU WILL NEED:
• A notebook or paper
• A pen

WHAT YOU WILL EXPERIENCE:
• A sense of fairness

1. Throughout one day, observe your actions and reactions, and write down how good or bad you felt when doing something. For example:

• You try to park the car, but curse and swear to yourself because you can't find a space. Do you judge your rage as a bad thing, or a good thing because you got your anger out of your system?

• You're in a supermarket queue and have a load of supplies to pay for, and an elderly lady has only one can of peas. You let her go in front of you and then feel virtuous and proud to be so kind. Do you judge this as good and true because you really do care about the elderly, or do you judge yourself as not so good after all, because you may have a darker motive for being a goody-goody?

• Maybe you get a call from a friend who tells you she's leaving her boyfriend, and at first you reassure her and tell her she's doing the right thing, but later you change your mind and decide she's in the wrong. Do you have an emotional investment in her situation? Why did you change your mind? Do you truly want what's best for her, or actually what is best for yourself?

2. Spend the rest of the day making these judgments.

3. In the evening look at your list, but step out of the role of judge and see your actions all from a neutral point of view with no invested goodness or badness. Now, you can experience being impartial, non-judgmental, and as fair as the lady with the scales herself.

THE HANGED MAN

KEYS

- Being in limbo
- Adjustment
- Changing priorities
- Paradox
- Looking at life from a different angle
- Taking one step back to move on
- Making a sacrifice

XII

THE HANGED MAN

MEANING

A man hangs from a tree by one foot; the other leg, bent at the knee, forms a triangle with his haloed head below. This mysterious card is one of the most complex and paradoxical of the Major Arcana. Marking about halfway through the Major Arcana, it requires anyone on their tarot journey to take a different viewpoint before they go on.

EXAMPLE INTERPRETATIONS

This card invites you to think about doing the opposite of what you believe is the right way to gain results, but it also can have a few varieties on this theme. Which is why it's important to learn and work with the Hanged Man from various "angles" just as its major symbol implies. In the "you now" position, you may be at a crossroads and need to stand back and take a good look at where you're going before you proceed. You may be in limbo or uncertain of what to do next, bored with life, or ready to give up something for something else. Sacrifice may be necessary, but are you being manipulated into doing so? As a future or outcome card, adjustment and reassessment of your plans will be needed, and as a blockage card your reluctance to take a different perspective on your life is what's actually holding you up.

A DIFFERENT VIEW OF LIFE

To help you to think out of the box or change your perception even though you are still "you," this exercise will literally make you see things upside down and back to front.

WHAT YOU WILL NEED:

- An outside, tranquil space, preferably in the countryside
- A compass
- Four white quartz crystals

WHAT YOU WILL EXPERIENCE:

- The Hanged Man's point of view

1. When you reach your quiet spot, take your compass and find out in which direction north lies. Place one crystal about two feet in front of you facing north, then do the same thing with the remaining three crystals, marking east, south, then west in that order to protect and invoke the power of the four directions which align to the four astrological elements.

2. Stand in the middle of the square of crystals, face north and bend over forwards, with legs well apart as if to touch your toes (only bend as much as you can so that your head is upside down). If you manage to see between your legs,

so much the better. Now for ten seconds imagine you are the Hanged Man, not very comfortable, but seeing south when in fact you are "facing north." You're actually in limbo, but seeing the paradoxical nature of life. Now, gradually unfurl your body, breathe deeply a few times to relax and unwind, then do the same thing to the east so that you are seeing west, while facing east.

3. Remain in this pose for a few seconds knowing that you have just hung out with the Hanged Man and understand his dilemma. That dilemma is yours too, but now you know how to deal with it by viewing life from a different angle.

DEATH

KEYS

- Change
- New beginnings
- One door closes, another opens
- Transformation
- Letting go of the past
- Finalizing unfinished business
- Cyclical nature of life

XIII

DEATH

MEANING

This deadly looking card isn't so bad after all, even though it's easy to see why it spooks most people—please don't take it literally. The armored skeleton, who represents "death," carries the motif of a rose on a flag symbolizing immortality, and beyond him is the rising sun, a sign of a new dawn, new beginnings, and the cycles of change. He heralds not physical death, but positive energy concerned with transition. This card always means that change is in the air. It can be personal change, such as giving up old bad habits or relationship patterns, or finding a better way to live.

EXAMPLE INTERPRETATIONS

When Death appears in the "you now" position, then you are either in the process of a major change, or you are about to take a leap of faith, start afresh, or are concerned about the consequences of any life changes. In the future or outcome position, then change is inevitable, and if you go with the flow it will become an important transition period when you'll learn much from your improved vitality and the new you. As a blockage card, Death reveals that you fear change, and this fear is stopping you from moving on or attaining your ambitions.

EMBRACING CHANGE

Many of us don't take to change kindly. We like the known and reliable, even if it is not a particularly happy place to be. This exercise will limber your mind up to see that change is about liberation.

WHAT YOU WILL NEED:

• A purpose or mission

WHAT YOU WILL EXPERIENCE:

• An ability to accept change

1. Think of a purpose or mission—it can be anything you like, from going out for essential errands; taking a breath of fresh air in the countryside; or visiting family. Whatever it is, make up your mind exactly where you are going and at what time. Plan your route, inform people of your timings and schedule, then get started.

2. As you go about your mission, suddenly change your mind to go somewhere else. It doesn't matter where, as long as it is not where you first planned to go. This change of mind may make you initially worried.

Will you upset others? Won't it be a shame not to be heading to your planned destination after all? However you change your mind, observe how you feel. Do your best not to manipulate or force anything as it won't help you enjoy the excitement brought on by change, and implies that you might well fear it.

This is the experience of the Death card. And one last thing, if you end up somewhere you didn't intend to go, you often find you're on a life-changing journey for the better.

TEMPERANCE

KEYS

- Moderation
- Blending of ideas
- Compromise
- Need for cooperation
- Healing energy
- Alchemical process

XIV

TEMPERANCE

MEANING

Medieval alchemists distilled strange potions, tried to turn lead into gold, and some even attempted to draw down the energies of the planets to become as powerful as the Universe. Temperance represents this blending—of stirring and mixing the right proportion of this or that to make your life harmonious and balanced. The angel is pouring liquid between two goblets, not only reminding you about the balance of mind, body, and spirit, or good relationships, but also to find a harmonious link between your desires and needs. Do they have the same purpose? Are they compatible?

EXAMPLE INTERPRETATIONS

This card implies it's time to merge ideas with others, or combine resources and plans to achieve harmony in your life. Your own inner "angel" is at work; you must listen to reason and to what your heart truly wants. Enjoy feeling centered and peaceful. As a "you now" card, your willingness to compromise without giving up your true desires will influence others. As a future card, you may have to juggle with needs and desires to create harmony in your life, but clarification of your goals is coming your way. As a blockage card, trying to please everyone else is the cause of any current problems.

HARMONY POTION

To truly understand this process of blending and mixing, you are going to make your own magic harmony potion.

WHAT YOU WILL NEED:

- Goblet or glass bowl
- A jug of natural spring water
- Five rose petals
- Essential oils of lavender, jasmine, and sandalwood

WHAT YOU WILL EXPERIENCE:

- The art of moderation

1. Sit before your table with the ingredients, and gently relax your mind by closing your eyes for about thirty seconds. Now pour some of the water into the goblet or bowl, filling it only about halfway.

2. Take the rose petals and sprinkle them onto the water as you make the following affirmation:

> *Through the blending of this potion, all harmony will come to my life and for those that I love.*

3. Now add five drops of each of the essential oils, and repeat the same affirmation as you do so.

4. Leave the potion for two nights and two days, by a window, to be infused with the energy of the sun and moon. Once ready, sprinkle drops of it around your entrance or front door, and also a few drops in your bedroom to bring harmony to your home and to those who enter there.

You will experience how blending ingredients can bring temperance to our lives.

THE DEVIL

KEYS

- Illusions
- Materialistic or sexual desires
- Living a lie
- Being obsessed
- Temptation
- Emotional bondage
- You as your own worst enemy

XV

THE DEVIL

MEANING

The Devil, rooted in a Greek word meaning "adversary," is actually our own worst enemy: oneself. It is that part of you who lives a lie, or believes that by having power, we can maintain control. The Devil card reveals we are overly dependent on material wealth, or obsessed with only one thing. In fact, our over attachment to something or someone actually controls us, making us powerless. This emotional bondage is represented by the two chained figures. If they just remove the chains, they will be free. Similarly, if we can detach ourselves from certain beliefs, then we are free from our illusions and can live a more fulfilling life.

EXAMPLE INTERPRETATIONS

In the "you now" position, the most simple interpretation is that you are attracted to someone for lust or money, or that you are obsessed with something and your illusions are preventing you from seeing the truth. In the blockage position, someone else's expectations or power trip is stopping you from seeing the light; don't be fooled by their charm. As an outcome or future card, be aware that you will have to battle against the temptations of sex or money to achieve happiness; don't be led astray by someone who wants to control you.

A BOX FULL OF ILLUSIONS

Possessions give us a sense of security, but sometimes we need to let go and see that not everything we treasure is of benefit to us. This exercise will help you to sort out what is worthless and what is truly hard to part with.

WHAT YOU WILL NEED:
- An empty shoe or cardboard box
- Pieces of paper
- A pen

WHAT YOU WILL EXPERIENCE:
- A sense that you can free yourself from the chains of illusion

1. Place your box and paper on a table and sit quietly. Relax and close your eyes to calm your mind for a few moments.

2. Take up your pen and write down all the things in your life that really matter to you, such as money, family, security, peace, and so on.

3. On a separate piece of paper, write the things that don't matter to you at all.

4. Compare the two lists, and check whether you have mistaken any of the items and put them in the wrong category. You may surprise yourself and find that some of the things in the "don't matter" list actually do matter to you.

5. Fold up the two pieces of paper and place the one that has the list of things that DO MATTER in the box, and close the lid.

6. Leave the box for a week under or near your bed, and each evening open it and reflect on whether these things really do matter to you, and if so why?

7. After a week, take the paper in the box, ceremoniously cut the page in pieces, and throw them away as recycled trash. Now you are throwing away the things that apparently do matter, but does this feel any different? Does it make you cringe to throw away the written words of the things you truly love, or are they just illusions, too? Think about it.

THE TOWER

KEYS

- External disruption
- Turmoil, upheaval
- Sudden change
- Unexpected challenges
- Breakdown and renewal
- Chaos all around
- Falling apart to fall together
- Shaking up, waking up

XVI

THE TOWER

MEANING

This "out of the blue" card is perhaps the most revolutionary card in the deck, signifying chaos, turmoil, and sometimes emphasizing a shocking personal experience. With the lightning strike comes breakdown and destruction, but also a breakthrough. It's as if the structure of our personal world is totally demolished, but there is now a chance to see the light and rebuild the "tower" in a creative and positive way. If you like to control your life, then the Tower can seem frightening or unsettling. The Tower also reminds us that we must recognize that sometimes we have to move forward and adapt to change.

EXAMPLE INTERPRETATIONS

In the "you now" position, this card means you are either in the middle of some crisis, or about to have a shake-up in your life; either way, it's a life-changing experience for the better. In the future or outcome position, unexpected events will make you question your outlook on life, and you will come to see a specific issue that you had previously been naive about in a new and creative light. As a blockage card, it means you are fearful of change. If you draw this card regularly, you need to recognize that sometimes things have to fall apart before they can fall together.

HAVE A RANT

Many of us don't like change, especially when it is apparently forced on us from outside circumstances. This exercise will help you to adjust to sudden change as if you were one moment in a raging temper, the next, cool, calm, and carefree.

WHAT YOU WILL NEED:

• A solitary place where you can make noise

WHAT YOU WILL EXPERIENCE:

• Unexpected change

For this exercise, you will need to be in a room or somewhere out in the countryside where no one can hear you.

1. Say everything out loud, even if you feel at first like a complete fool. Say exactly what you hate or loathe about anything—friends, family, partners, or colleagues. Get totally angry and wind yourself up with it. Shout out, swear and curse if necessary, to make you confident in your little rant. Get raving mad and shout and act like a toddler. You can even stamp your feet, bang around or just pummel the cushions. Get out that anger!

2. Suddenly stop. Listen to the silence, as sudden and as unexpected as the Tower's influence. The sudden change from wild to civilized, the noise to stillness, these are all similar to the lightning strike of the card. In the stillness, there is peace and a realization that unexpected change can be beneficial.

THE STAR

KEYS

- Inspiration
- Truth revealed
- Manifesting a dream
- Seeing the light
- Insight and self-belief
- Ideal love

XVII

THE STAR

MEANING

The Star offers peace, inspiration, and direct experience of how the Universe can come to your aid by bringing creative ideas and a surge of personal fulfillment. The eight stars on the card represent the eight planets of astrology—Mercury, Venus, Mars, Jupiter, Saturn, Neptune, Uranus, and Pluto—which have their own individual tarot cards. When they are in harmonious alignment they will bring you great joy. The naked nymph pours water from two jugs symbolizing that the balance is now right for you to proceed and create your own opportunities.

EXAMPLE INTERPRETATIONS

In all layouts, this card is hugely beneficial and usually signifies great success, abundant aspirations, and fulfillment in relationships, business or career issues. In the "you now" position, the Star reveals your optimistic attitude and your ability to make use of your talents. As a future card, the Star suggests that you're going to manifest a dream, or that a revelation will bring you the rewards you seek. It can also indicate a new or flourishing love affair. As a blockage card, the Star shows that you may not be able to live up to your high expectations of yourself, or that your future plans are too idealistic.

THE MUSIC OF THE SPHERES

Being at one with the cosmos even for a few moments is exhilarating. What better way to do it than by looking up to the stars themselves and being in tune with the music of the spheres?

WHAT YOU WILL NEED:
• A view of the night sky (either literally standing beneath the stars, or an image of the sky)
• Two crystals

WHAT YOU WILL EXPERIENCE:
• A sense of universal empowerment

1. During the evening when all is dark apart from the twinkling stars (unless of course you live with light pollution or a permanently cloudy sky), go outside and find a special place to sit and look up to the heavens. If you're doing this with an image, use candlelight in the room, just enough for you to see the image before you.

2. Place the two crystals in your lap, and then close your eyes and imagine yourself as a twinkling star up there in space with the other stars. Open your eyes and now gaze at the constellations. You may make out some you know, or you might even see a shooting star, but whatever the case imagine the whole cosmos is in harmony. You might even find yourself humming or whistling a tune.

3. Take the two crystals, one in each hand, and focus on their vibratory force and their connection to the harmony of the stars themselves.

4. After several minutes, open your eyes, replace the crystals in your lap, and relax. You will now understand that the infinite nature of yourself is what the Star card really represents.

THE MOON

KEYS

- Illusion
- Self-deceit
- Blind to the truth
- Hanging on to the past
- Confusion
- Loss
- Imagination
- Intuition

XVIII

THE MOON

MEANING

The Moon is deceptive and yet alight with intuitive wisdom. It often carries a warning that you are losing yourself in your worries. But this also enables you to plunder the depths of your unconscious so you can deal with your projected fears in a positive way. The moon casts a false light (the light reflected by the sun) on the earth, particularly when it's full. When we are overcome by personal loss or a sense of vulnerability, it's hard to know what to do. This is the Moon's territory, reminding us that we need to trust our inner voice, which may be lost beneath secret motives and hidden truths. We also need to turn negative thinking into positive attributes.

EXAMPLE INTERPRETATIONS

As a "you now" card, things may not be all they seem. Your judgment may be unsound, or someone may be taking advantage of you. Listen to your intuition and don't deceive yourself about the truth. As a future or outcome card, any illusion you now have will be brought to the surface—someone will try to manipulate you or hidden information will come to light. As a blockage card, the Moon indicates it's your insecurity or sense of loss that is holding you back in your current quest.

DARK AND LIGHT

Understanding that you have a dark side as well as a vibrant light side helps you to accept your faults as well as nurture your virtues. This exercise allows you to see how the Moon represents your shadow.

WHAT YOU WILL NEED:
- A piece of A4 paper
- Black and white artist paint
- Brush and palette

WHAT YOU WILL EXPERIENCE:
- Your own lunar landscape

You don't have to be an artist or even an aspiring one to do this exercise, but it will make you understand how in every dark corner, there is light to be found too.

1. Place a large blob of black paint on the left side of your palette and a large blob of white paint on the right side.

2. Next, paint about half the paper black and half white (as shown in the diagram). Now mix some of the black paint with a bit of white paint on your palette to make a dark gray. Paint this like a large round circle on the line where the black and white meet.

You now have a gray area where the black and white meet; it is here that consciousness meets unconsciousness, where you can work with the illusions created by vulnerability and fear, and as you gaze for a while at your work of art, you realize that the dark side of the moon is part of the light side too. They are one, as you can see from your "gray area."

 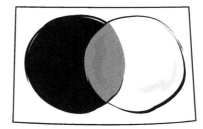

THE SUN

KEYS

- Joy
- Positive energy
- Accomplishment in love
- Creativity and growth
- Happiness
- Enlightenment
- Being the center of attention

THE SUN

MEANING

This card represents all that brings us joy to feed our ego. Without the sun there would be no life on earth. The card reveals the power of the Sun as it shines down on a happy child with golden hair riding a white horse, representing our own inner fulfillment when things go right for us. The Sun also symbolizes courage, victory, and emotional clarity. If the Moon represents the veil of self-deception, the Sun reminds us to live life to the full, to revel in our vitality. When you draw this card, you can take center stage and leave your shadows behind.

EXAMPLE INTERPRETATIONS

Whatever this card's position, it is a positive card and urges you to act. As a "you now" card, you're brimming over with ideas and happy thoughts, and if not, well, it's time to play with life. You can accept others for who they are, rather than trying to change them. As a future card, you can expect fun-loving moments, and be liberated from any doubt or fear. It also signifies that a playful, romantic relationship may begin, allowing you to become the focus of attention. As a blockage card, you are exaggerating your happiness, or you're concerned with your image, but you can't communicate your need to have fun and be seen as someone special.

A SOLAR DAY

The sun rises and then sets according to our view of it from earth, so here you can be the sun from dawn to dusk to experience the joy of solar power.

WHAT YOU WILL NEED:
- A gold-colored ring
- A gold-colored necklace
- A piece of citrine of golden topaz

WHAT YOU WILL EXPERIENCE:
- Being special like the sun

1. Put on the gold necklace and ring, and carry the piece of citrine with you in your bag or pocket; wear any other golden regalia you might have.

2. Go about your daily business and consciously smile at a stranger when you know they are looking at you. This smile has to come deep from within you, saying "you are a lovely person" or "you're beautiful." Did you feel cheeky, playful, fun-loving? Or did you cringe at the thought the stranger wouldn't smile back?

3. As you carry on with your day, feel the power of the citrine and the gold working their magic.

4. If you manage to find the sun shining down upon you, turn your face to the sky (don't look at the sun directly) and thank the sun for bringing you radiance so that you stand out from the crowd and feel the joy that is the world.

5. At the end of the day, take off your regalia and return to normal, knowing that you are special and just as vibrant as the sun.

JUDGMENT

KEYS

- Epiphany
- Awakening
- Liberation and rebirth
- Reevaluation and revival
- Accepting things as they are
- Putting the past behind you
- Judging with forgiveness
- Seeing the truth of the matter

XX

JUDGMENT

MEANING

The word "judge" is rooted in a Latin word meaning "to form an opinion." This card is concerned with forming an opinion, then acting upon it. This can arise as a "calling"—a new vocation or an awakening, such as liberation from the chains of a terrible relationship—or simply an acceptance that you can now be reborn and freed. We see in the card the angel Gabriel calling on the dead to rise and be liberated from their mortal state. In fact, the angel is trumpeting out the news that the Universe holds the key to help you reevaluate your life and to fulfill your true potential.

EXAMPLE INTERPRETATIONS

In the "you now" position, Judgment implies you are in the process of making a decision to change your lifestyle in some way and wake up to who you truly are. It can also imply that you are liberating yourself from the past, ready to confront unfinished business, clear up misunderstandings, and know deep within the right pathway for you. In the future or outcome positions, let the past go and you will stop feeling guilty or nostalgic for what has been. Soon you will be able to make a life-changing decision. As a blockage card, you may feel judged by others or are blaming yourself for someone else's troubles.

LETTING GO

This exercise will help you to work with this complex card and realize that life is about acting on your opinions, rather than judging others according to that opinion.

WHAT YOU WILL NEED:
- Twelve stones or pebbles
- An outdoor space

WHAT YOU WILL EXPERIENCE:
- A sense of liberation

1. For this exercise, it's important that you actively go out into the countryside or somewhere where you can find pebbles, stones, or even shells (a beach is perfect too) and gather up twelve stones that "speak" to you.

2. When you have your twelve special pebbles, go and sit quietly somewhere, still in the same environment. If possible, sit cross-legged with the pebbles either in a pouch placed between your legs, or in the lap of your skirt (if you happen to be wearing one!).

3. Now relax, close your eyes, and concentrate on one thing you'd truly like to do in the future. Take one pebble at a time from the bag and as you chuck it back to its home ground, repeat the following affirmation:

Begone the stones of the past. I am awakening to who I really am.

4. Say this each time you remove and throw out a pebble, until you have one left. This pebble represents the future, and you can now move on without blame or anger. Keep this pebble with you—it won't judge you.

THE WORLD

KEYS

- Culmination
- Completion
- Fulfillment
- Feeling at one with the Universe
- Reward
- Accomplishment
- Travel (both physical and mental)
- Father Time

XXI

THE WORLD

MEANING

The World symbolizes not only fulfillment of one's wishes and goals, but how you are "whole," self-aware, and integrated. This card implies a sense of accomplishment and prosperity, and acclaim for those who deserve it. The World "picks up" on themes and symbols from earlier cards, such as the four elements shown on the Wheel of Fortune. The goddess dances through the heavens, her left knee bent, creating a triangle, similar to the Hanged Man's stance. The wreath surrounding the goddess is tied with two infinity symbols, showing that the World card "pulls together all that is," so that the Fool can at last come home.

EXAMPLE INTERPRETATIONS

As a "you now" card, you have found your direction and can be sure of whatever plans you put into motion. The outcome will be perfect. It can also imply that a long-term project has come full circle and you are now feeling a sense of closure and accomplishment. The World also implies that you are in the right place, doing the right thing and feeling fulfilled. As a future or outcome card, it heralds new, fulfilling beginnings. As a blockage card, you may be too sure of yourself, and need to ask yourself some straight questions.

UNPACK YOUR BAG

The Fool's journey is complete and it's time to unpack your backpack. If the World is about fulfillment, then this exercise reveals not only how you can feel at one with the cosmos, but also at one with yourself.

WHAT YOU WILL NEED:
• The backpack drawing

WHAT YOU WILL EXPERIENCE
• Being part of the tarot

You've come full circle—the Fool in you stepped off into the big wide world, met up with other mirror images of yourself, and has now come to understand that with self-awareness, you can become the complete version of yourself, fulfilled to your potential.

1. Take the Fool's backpack paper from the box or drawer. Unfold it and look at the five items that you listed for your journey. Do they still convey the same message, invoke the same feelings? If any have changed, or are no longer relevant, strike them off your list. Unpack your bag completely if you like; you may see things from a different perspective than when you began. If not, you may have to do a little more work on yourself.

2. Reflect for a while and consider your own tarot journey so far (as it's not over yet!). Has it been easier than you imagined? Or has it taken you into a world you'd rather not have gazed at?

The Fool in you can now face the true Self and realize that you have the power to connect to the mystical nature of the Universe, because you are part of it. For the next stage of your journey, you're going to meet a whole host of other characters, but for now, fold the paper up and replace it in the box until later.

CHAPTER THREE

THE KEY
to the
MINOR
ARCANA

- ○─➤ The Minor Arcana are about everyday experiences

- ○─➤ The four suits correspond to the four elements

- ○─➤ The court cards can represent people we meet

- ○─➤ The number cards resonate to the music of the spheres

INTRODUCTION TO THE MINOR ARCANA

So, now you've worked in depth with each of the Major Arcana cards, and you should feel as if you're beginning to understand and experience each card's archetype. The Major Arcana as we've seen are mirrors of all the Universe that is in you, and the journey you take to get there. But what about the Minor Arcana?

The Minor Arcana are made up of fifty-six cards. Each of the four suits is made up of fourteen cards. Though they do not carry the quintessential archetypes of the Major Arcana cards, think of them as practical, day-to-day events, people, and short-term influences, which can lead you to the deeper truths of the Major Arcana in any reading. The four astrological elements are Fire, Earth, Air, and Water and correspond to the suits as shown in the table below, along with each element's associated qualities. The elements each have three associated star signs.

ELEMENT	SUIT	QUALITIES	STAR SIGNS
Fire	Wands	Creativity Inspiration Action	Leo Sagittarius Aries
Earth	Pentacles	Substance Reality Calculation	Taurus Virgo Capricorn
Air	Swords	State of mind Reason Logic	Gemini Libra Aquarius
Water	Cups	Feeling Emotion Intensity	Cancer Scorpio Pisces

MATCHING THE NUMBERS
AND THE SUITS

Numbers are also mystical symbols that resonate to the vibrations of the cosmos. Use this brief guide to numbers to help you when interpreting numbered cards, and adapt the interpretation according to the suit.

1. Write down the following numbers and their corresponding qualities. Then by association, add your own words to the list. So, for example, Unity becomes Wholeness, Oneness, and so on.

> **Ace or One**—Unity becomes…
> **Two**—Negotiation becomes…
> **Three**—Communication becomes…
> **Four**—Stability becomes…
> **Five**—Versatility becomes…
> **Six**—Harmony becomes…
> **Seven**—Intuition becomes…
> **Eight**—Manifestation becomes…
> **Nine**—Action becomes…
> **Ten**—Beginnings, endings, and fulfillment become…

2. Now you need to put together the "number" with the "suit" to blend the qualities together.

   For example, take the number eight and add it to the suit of Wands, putting together the keywords "manifestation" with "inspiration and action." What do these words mean to you personally? Think about them together—how could you rearrange them or change them to make a sentence?

3. Next, take a look at the eight of Wands card. Eight wands are flying through the air as if thrown by an unknown person. There is a feeling of movement, swift action, and nothing is grounded, only speculative. Then add "you" into the equation. A positive interpretation would be that you are rushing ahead, driven by flashes of insight to manifest a goal.

   Alternatively, it could mean you're so driven by your ideas that everything is up in the air and you can't get anything done. It all depends on you and how your intuition works with a card.

THE COURT CARDS

The four court cards, Page, Knight, Queen, and King, usually represent people you meet in everyday life, who are signposts on your journey or influences in your life. They may be people you already know, or strangers. They can also be aspects of your own personality, which you may project, unknowingly, onto others. For example, you may fall in love with a rebellious type because they seem so different from you, but you are unaware of that quality within yourself.

So whether the Mother Earth type (Queen of Pentacles) or the gallant rogue (Knight of Wands), the court cards are both a mirror of your own inner world, or people "out there" who awaken or reflect certain parts of you.

The rank of the court card will also give you a clue as to the kind of energy expressed by yourself or the people around you.

KINGS

All four Kings represent power and extrovert energy. They may sit on thrones, but they are ready to act or make crucial decisions. They symbolize dynamic energy, and they also represent maturity and authority figures.

QUEENS

The Queens symbolize the power of the feminine. These qualities include protection, receptivity, nurturing, intuition, and female authority figures. Queens are all about creative energy and passive power.

KING

WANDS

QUEEN

SWORDS

KNIGHT

PENTACLES

PAGE

CUPS

KNIGHTS

The most difficult of court cards to interpret, Knights represent the suit's quality at its worst and its best—in other words, the extremes of energy of the suit. For example, the Knight of Wands is seductive and charming, but totally insensitive. Knights can also represent friends or lovers.

PAGES

Page energy is playful, lighthearted, and lively. They can appear in your life as young adults, childish lovers, jovial spirits, or literally children. They also represent opportunists or your own immature attitude.

GETTING TO KNOW THE COURT CARDS

1. To get acquainted with the court cards, separate them from the deck so you have four Pages, four Knights, four Queens, and four Kings. Lay them out in four rows so the Pages are on the top row, the Knights on the next row, then the Queens, then the Kings at the bottom row.

2. Look at the four Pages together and try to imagine what kind of people they represent. You know that Pages are about childish, lighthearted energy, so how would these characters show up in your life? You know Wands are about creativity and action, so what kind of Page is the Page of Wands?

3. Before you look up my interpretations on the following pages, take a few minutes or so to write down what you think all these court cards represent. Write just one simple sentence for each. For example, the Queen of Pentacles: "Warm-hearted and caring mother figure."

4. Once you have a phrase for each, you can begin to add more words or ideas that come to you as you work through the rest of the Minor Arcana. So before you start turning to the interpretation pages, the next thing you're going to learn is how to get to know and experience the four suits individually.

THE SUIT OF WANDS

KEYS

- ○—× Fire
- ○—× Energy
- ○—× Will
- ○—× Desire
- ○—× Drive
- ○—× Competition
- ○—× Boldness
- ○—× Egotism
- ○—× Hot-tempered

MEANING

Wands (also known as Scepters, Rods, Batons, and Staffs) are usually depicted as long fiery brands, staves, or tree branches (as in the Rider-Waite and Universal decks) with sprouting leaf shoots, which represent new growth and the spark of life.

Like the Fire signs—Aries, Leo, and Sagittarius—Wands signify vision, intention, and a goal-oriented outlook on life. Fire and Wands are looking to the future, never to the past. This suit describes how we actively engage in life on a daily basis; the creative process and how we initiate and act upon that creative idea or scheme. If you find you draw a majority of Wands in a reading, it suggests you're impatient for results or for an adventure, or that you're taking on too much too soon, depending on the "focus" card (see pages 134–135).

Most of the Wands show people seeking, contemplating, or engaged in action. These are energizing, motivational cards, so they are always interpreted as moving towards a goal rather than having reached one—active rather than passive.

MEET THE WANDS COURT CARDS

WHAT YOU WILL NEED:

• A piece of paper
• A pen
• The Wands court cards

WHAT YOU WILL EXPERIENCE:

• The drive and motivation of the suit of Wands

1. Remove the Wands court cards from the deck and place them in a row—Page, Knight, Queen, King—on the piece of paper.

2. Under each card, write the name of someone you know who might "fit" or identify with the relevant court cards. For example, the Queen of Wands looks sure of herself, accompanied by her "familiar" black cat—does this character remind you of someone you know?

3. Next, imagine you have invited these court card personalities to a party. How would each of the characters approach the buffet table? For example, would the King march up and take what he wanted before anyone else, or would he lead by example and politely wait for the Queen to make up her mind?

The whole thing about the court cards is that with a little imagination, association, and an understanding of character, you can build some powerful images around these people. The main thing about Fire signs, and therefore "Wands people," is that they're pushy, self-confident, and proactive.

4. Finally, write down below each card how they would leave the party; just a couple of words is enough. You can have fun with this, stating things such as "by the bathroom window," "in a rush," or "with a flourish."

5. Now, do you feel comfortable around these pushy people? Do you find you can easily identify with their nature, or do you find it irritating? Record your feelings on the same paper.

THE WANDS COURT CARDS

These are only suggested interpretations for the court cards, but however brief, they will help you to build up a picture of these characters and their role in your life.

PAGE

WANDS

KNIGHT

WANDS

QUEEN

WANDS

KING

WANDS

PAGE OF WANDS

KEYS

- Creative ideas
- Fresh insight
- A charming admirer
- Childlike exuberance
- Showing enthusiasm

The Page of Wands is similar to the Fool in that he is willing to leap in at the deep end, but unlike the Fool's careless disregard for the outcome, the Page has the confidence to focus on what will happen next. If the question is concerned with love, then this card represents a younger admirer, a seductive charmer, or fun and games. In the "you now" position, the Page reveals you are full of enthusiasm, and you have fresh insight into your choices. As a future or outcome card, you are about to enter a period of fun and optimism. As a blockage card, your enthusiasm is stopping you from seeing how to make progress.

KNIGHT OF WANDS

KEYS

- Passionate, but impetuous
- Adventurous, but unreliable
- Accomplished, but exaggerates the truth
- Enthusiastic, but makes empty promises
- Charming, but insensitive

The Knights represent extremes of energy, as you can see from the keywords. These traits can be seen as either positive or negative depending on your situation. This card is all about vivacity and daring. It might also refer literally to a "knight in shining armor," who comes into your life to seduce you. In the "you now" position, it's time to be reckless and express your daring or seductive streak. In the blockage position, you're infatuated with someone who won't settle down. As a future or outcome card, look forward to excitement, adventures, or freedom-loving individuals coming into your life.

QUEEN OF WANDS
KEYS
- Charismatic and creative
- Sexually accomplished
- Attractive
- A self-assured female
- Confident and optimistic

When you draw this card, fiery, challenging, or highly creative females are influences in your life. So, for example, in the blockage position, there is a woman in your business, family, or social circle who is stopping you from moving on. In the "you now" position, you're upbeat and magnetic, so be as attractive and self-assured as you want. As a future card, you will be able to make an important impression when needed. Your charismatic nature will bring you the opportunity or success you're looking for.

KING OF WANDS
KEYS
- Powerful and dramatic
- Inspirational authority figure
- Theatrical and bold
- Role model
- Showcase performance

The King of Wands suggests the energy is dramatic and vibrant in whatever you do. This fiery king often appears as a male leader or authority figure, who is talented and charismatic. As a "you now" card, you can now draw on all your wisdom and insight to forge ahead with your plans. You have a larger-than-life attitude, so go out and do what you know best. In the blockage position, power issues must be addressed before you can achieve anything, or a male authority figure is challenging you as a rival. In the future, you will be able to mastermind your goals, and it's your own inspiration that will help you succeed.

THE WANDS NUMBER CARDS

The Wands number cards show how we initiate experiences. Whether we are plotting our future or battling with others, these cards are symbols of our daily activity.

| I | II | III | IV | V |

ACE OF WANDS
KEYS
- Fresh start
- Creative vision,
- Acting on an idea
- Knowing the right way forward

As Wands are about action, this card signifies that you have to get something done. It is not about just thinking inspiring thoughts, but acting upon them. In the "you now" position, it's timely to go ahead with your plans. In the outcome or future position, exciting opportunities will come your way. In the blockage position, be aware that your expectations aren't too high.

TWO OF WANDS
KEYS
- Personal power
- Pioneering spirit
- Seizing the moment
- Showing you mean business

Two is the number of doubling strength; combining the energies to conquer or achieve something. This card makes you feel as if you're capable of anything. But take care in the blockage position that you're not feeling invincible. As a future card, you're about to persuade others of your talents.

THREE OF WANDS
KEYS
- ○→ Foresight
- ○→ Exploration
- ○→ Starting a new journey
- ○→ Seeking the truth
- ○→ Having an open mind

Just like the figure on the card, there's no looking back when you draw this card in the "you now" position. Prepare yourself for a new departure, but give yourself time to reflect on what is on offer. In the blockage position, you're concentrating only on the future so that you're missing the truth of the present. As a future card, you will soon be off on a fascinating exploration—in work, love, or just the world at large.

FOUR OF WANDS
KEYS
- ○→ Joy
- ○→ Celebration
- ○→ Preparing for a happy event
- ○→ Feeling proud
- ○→ Domestic harmony

It is a key period for celebration when you draw this card in the "you now" position. Time to tidy up the home, declutter, enjoy family life, or simply have fun. As a blockage card, you're more concerned with your social life than your self-development, and as a future card, lively people, social events, and celebrations are all good influences.

FIVE OF WANDS
KEYS
- ○→ Minor setbacks
- ○→ Rivalry
- ○→ Disagreement and discord
- ○→ Frustrating events
- ○→ Competition

From harmony and social grace, we all inevitably encounter friction too. In the "you now" position, everyone seems to be attacking your viewpoint, or the world seems against you. As a blockage card, you're trying too hard to win. In the future, you may be at odds with yourself, and what you think you want may not be what you truly need.

THE WANDS NUMBER CARDS: PART ONE

1. Place the five cards shown on this spread in a line. Imagine that you are going to a job interview; think of what each card would imply or represent for each of the five days leading up to the interview.

2. Write down a keyword and then an intuitive sentence on a piece of paper, and see how your story unfolds.

VI	VII	VIII	IX	X

WANDS	WANDS	WANDS	WANDS	WANDS

SIX OF WANDS

KEYS

- Victory
- Pride
- Feeling superior
- Taking it all in stride
- Reputation

When you draw this in the "you now" position, you are certainly proving you have succeeded and deserve public acclaim. However, beware that you don't get an inflated ego. As a blockage card, your superiority complex is getting in the way of your true path. As a future card, you're soon to be victorious and be the center of attention.

SEVEN OF WANDS

KEYS

- Defiance
- Being resolute
- Standing your ground
- Struggling to prove yourself
- Continued rivalry

The soldier has lost one of his leg armor plates, suggesting he's still not perfected his trade, and he is in a constant struggle against rivals who want to take his place. But as a "you now" card, with perseverance and determination, you will win against your adversaries. As a blockage card, you're having a battle with your conscience or others about making a decision. As a future card, you will have to prepare yourself to fight any opposition to your plans.

EIGHT OF WANDS

KEYS

- Taking swift action
- Resolving unfinished business
- Getting your priorities sorted
- Completion of a project

Fast and furious flying wands are approaching the earth, ready to hit the ground. As a "you now" card, if you act quickly, you can accomplish a lot in a short time. As a blockage card, you need to come down to earth and be realistic about your ideas. As a future card, you can expect a busy and exciting time ahead of you; tasks will get completed if you're organized and pursue the right opportunities.

NINE OF WANDS

KEYS

- Resilience
- Persistence
- Prepared for anything
- Defending yourself
- Test of self-belief

In the "you now" position, you feel exhausted even though you've nearly achieved your goals, but there is one last test or challenge before you can reach ultimate success. You are in a position of strength, and the last obstacle will be overcome. In the blockage position, you're expecting the worst to happen rather than being positive. As a future card, your resilience will pay off.

TEN OF WANDS

KEYS

- Uphill struggle
- Heavy burden
- Too much responsibility
- Struggling with workload

In the "you now" position, you have fulfilled a creative venture, realized a dream, or accomplished a major goal. However, with the achievement of your goal comes greater responsibilities,

and these can be a burden to you. Examine your current goals, lifestyle, and workload; delegate if necessary. As a blockage card, it's your willingness to become a workhorse for everyone else that's stopping you from moving on.

THE WANDS NUMBER CARDS: PART TWO

1. Take the five cards shown on this spread, and as before, place them in a line starting from the Six of Wands, across to the Ten of Wands. This time, imagine you got the job that you interviewed for in the last exercise. What do these cards reveal about the next five weeks (one card for each week)?

2. Use one keyword to interpret each card as if it were an influence for a whole week, then write an intuitive phrase that comes to you to sum up the story of your first five weeks at your new job.

THE SUIT OF PENTACLES

KEYS

- Reality
- The senses
- Ownership
- Security
- Manifestation
- Worth

MEANING

Sometimes called Discs or Coins, the suit of Pentacles represents the tangible aspects of our life. Like the astrological Earth signs—Taurus, Virgo, and Capricorn—Pentacles are concerned with our personal resources and the substance of our physical selves.

Most modern decks based on the Rider-Waite deck depict the pentacle itself as a five-pointed star on a golden disc. A pentacle is a magic talisman used to invoke the power of spirits or deities in spell work. So although pentacles relate to the mundane world, they are also about the ability to manifest the dreams, ideas, and goals of all the other three suits. Pentacles also mirror the outer situations of your health, finances, work, and creativity. They have to do with how we see the external world, as well as how we create, shape, transform, and develop it.

If you draw a majority of pentacles in any spread, it's likely that things like money, business, security, and what you "own" are big issues for you at the moment. However, it can mean that you are resourceful at the expense of your spiritual or emotional needs, so care must be taken to adjust the balance.

MEET THE PENTACLES
COURT CARDS

WHAT YOU WILL NEED:
• The four Pentacles court cards
• A piece of paper (or your journal)
• A pen

WHAT YOU WILL EXPERIENCE:
• Your interaction with the material world

1. Place the four court cards on the table before you, with the Page at the left, then the Knight, Queen, and King.

2. Imagine that you are a wealthy business tycoon and you have four candidates for four very different jobs, and you have to decide which job would be best filled by each of the people before you.

3. Read the job descriptions below and then match who you think will best fit each job. Try not to look up the interpretations yet! Just observe the cards and use your intuition to understand the roles these court cards might be best suited for. The job vacancies:
• Financial director
• HR (human resources) manager
• Creative or hi-tech whiz kid
• Risk management adviser

4. Once you've sorted out who you think is whom (of course, there is no "right" answer, as obviously you're going to invest your own "Pentacle self" into the cards), decide how much value "YOU," as the wealthy business tycoon, place on each of the people and their jobs. For example, you might be a more "creative" type and think the development of the hi-tech world is more important than the risky business side of your company and so on.

5. Do you identify with any of these characters at all? Can you understand their "take" on life? Whatever you feel about them, write down the names of anyone you know who might personify these qualities. Then, turn to the interpretation pages to reveal more about the court cards.

THE PENTACLES COURT CARDS

The court cards are proud of their achievements. They appear quietly confident and ready to show they mean business.

PAGE	KNIGHT	QUEEN	KING

PENTACLES	PENTACLES	PENTACLES	PENTACLES

THE PAGE OF PENTACLES
KEYS
- Diligence
- Creative approach
- Practical aims
- Setting the wheels in motion
- A whiz kid

A young man stands alone in an open landscape; he is so focused on the pentacle in his hands, he's ready to leave the countryside and follow a goal. The card signifies the initial process of manifesting your dream rather than having completed it. In the "you now" position, you're ready to turn your visions into reality, or to "get on with the job" even if the question surrounds a relationship issue. As a blockage card, because you are so focused on your goals, you might miss your real priorities. As a future card, the Page can appear in your life as a whiz kid, a creative guru, or a friend with practical "know-how."

KNIGHT OF PENTACLES
KEYS
- Persistent
- Hardworking
- Conservative
- Unadventurous
- Realistic
- Dedicated
- Inflexible, but gets things done

The Knight rides a horse whose pricked-up ears suggest there's something in the distance that may be dangerous. The Knight immediately senses this and carries his compass-like disc to find a safe direction. Similarly, when you draw this as a "you now" card it implies it's time to knuckle down and get on with the job; don't fear the effort involved, it will pay off. Though the Knight's visions may not be earth-shattering, and his methods not original, he sees that everything he does will meet with success. As a future card, the Knight can appear in your life as someone who has the patience to accomplish tasks.

QUEEN OF PENTACLES
KEYS
- Resourceful
- Trustworthy
- Dependable
- Nurturing
- Generous
- Caring and warm-hearted

This kindly looking Queen holds her pentacle as if it were a child—careful, and with understanding. Similarly, this card is about the way we go about caring for our possessions, money, and business contacts. As a "you now" card, the Queen points a finger at you and asks the following: Where's your nurturing side? Do you look after yourself, or just others, or both? Are you able to remain a dependable friend, lover, or employee? In a blockage position, you may be caring so much for others at the expense of your own emotional needs. As a future card,

the Queen can appear in your life as a colleague, friend, or stranger who embodies the dependable, generous qualities that you may lack in your own life.

KING OF PENTACLES
KEYS
- Reliable
- Materialistic
- Enterprising
- Philanthropic
- Knowledgeable

This King has a bit of the Midas touch. In fact, he proudly shows off his pentacle to the busy world, surrounded by the glitz of the big city. This is one happy King. He's proud of his achievements and has reached the top of his tree. As a "you now" card, you have all the right instincts to succeed at any venture, or you're in a successful period of your life, so don't give up on it now. Enjoy what you have or are doing, and show you mean business. As a blockage card, you may be so obsessed with your business world that your relationships are suffering, and as a future card, a charismatic business or financial adviser will be a stabilizing influence on you.

THE PENTACLES NUMBER CARDS

The Pentacles number cards depict people getting on with their business, and others struggling or making money. These cards symbolize how we manifest Wands' goals.

ACE OF PENTACLES

KEYS

- Prosperity
- Abundance
- Being focused and grounded

In the "you now" position, it can imply you're turning over a new leaf and seeing how to invest in yourself. As a future card, prosperity is coming your way, as long as you stay grounded. As a blockage card, material gain means a lot to you, but temper it with spiritual development too.

TWO OF PENTACLES

KEYS

- Flexibility
- Balance
- Open to change
- Juggling with the options
- Sure of your skills

Our easygoing juggler has balanced his two pentacles by looping the infinity sign around them. When we're in tune with the Universe, we go with the flow. In the "you now" position, it's time to believe in yourself, lighten up, and take life less seriously. In the future, life's going to be easier to deal with, and in the blockage position, you might be taking on too much and need a rest.

THREE OF PENTACLES

KEYS

- Teamwork
- Cooperation
- Getting the job done
- Being aware of your talents

When you draw this card, even though you may be in the mood to go it alone, this is a time to share the load with others. Don't turn away help when it's on offer. As a blockage card, you're seeking approval by conforming, so maybe it's time to be a bit of a rebel? As a future card, be proud of what you're about to achieve and prove your place in the hierarchy. Your team spirit will bring you recognition and growth.

FOUR OF PENTACLES
KEYS
- Possessive
- Mean
- Greedy
- Material manipulation
- Resistant to change

The crowned man guards his pentacles in a miserly way—the Four of Pentacles indicates the temptation of valuing money above its real worth. This extreme attachment to the material world can damage good relationships. In the "you now" position, you are either controlling others with money or possessions, or you need to let go a little of the fears that come with ownership. You may have been in a difficult situation, but you can now create some material order in your world.

FIVE OF PENTACLES
KEYS
- Lack
- Rejection
- Hardship
- Victim mentality
- Neglecting your needs

This card indicates a sense of "lack" in your life. This card often turns up when we feel life has let us down, or we've become a victim in some way. If you feel your life is lacking something, then you must discover what it is rather than always seeing the glass half-empty. In the future, you may feel left out in the cold, but the only person who can warm you up is yourself—you must take responsibility.

THE PENTACLES NUMBER CARDS: PART ONE

1. Take the first five Pentacles number cards, and place them in a line on the table in front of you. Working from the Five of Pentacles to the Ace, write down one keyword that stands out for you for each card (the reason will be explained in the next exercise).

2. Then, write a few sentences that describe and sum up the story of how you arrive at the Ace, where after the gloom of the Five of Pentacles card, there is a new beginning.

VI	VII	VIII	IX	X
PENTACLES	PENTACLES	PENTACLES	PENTACLES	PENTACLES

SIX OF PENTACLES

KEYS

- Having and not having
- Loss and gain
- Domination and submission
- Generosity

This is a complex card concerned with the giving and receiving of financial benefits, or even love. Think, are you the giver or the receiver? This card asks us to reflect on the fact that sometimes in our gains we lose, and vice versa. What are your motivations for giving? Is someone buying your love? In the blockage position, you need to be especially vigilant about which side of the coin you are on.

SEVEN OF PENTACLES

KEYS

- Assessment
- Evaluation
- Seeing fruits of labor
- What next?

The gardener seems content with his work. He has a good harvest, but what to do with it? When you draw this as a "you now" card, it's time to take a step back and make an assessment. We need to know when to put down tools and stop. We may fear completion because it implies another new beginning. As a blockage card, don't sit around waiting for results—it's time to act.

EIGHT OF PENTACLES

KEYS

- Discipline
- Proficiency
- Diligence
- Getting to the nitty-gritty
- Repetitive situation

This card reminds you to get on with the job. It can also mean you're bogged down in repetitive work, but the results will pay off. As a blockage card, you may have reached a level where things are too easy, and it's time to accept you need a new challenge.

NINE OF PENTACLES
KEYS
- Accomplishment
- Independence
- Being resourceful
- Self-discipline

This card reveals that your recent efforts are the key to your future success. You have an inner sense of security and can now enjoy the finer pleasures of life. Your most important duty is to yourself, and like the falcon, who can fly away but usually comes back, you too are free to do as you please as long as you stay down to earth. As a blockage card, you wonder if there is anything in life left to achieve.

TEN OF PENTACLES
KEYS
- The good life
- Seeking affluence
- Enjoying abundance
- Conventional values

Whenever you draw this card, you need to ask yourself: What are my values and expectations? Are these expectations mine or someone else's? Do I really want affluence over and above anything else? It can also mean that, yes, you will enjoy the good life, and you have a right to it like anyone else.

THE PENTACLES NUMBER CARDS: PART TWO

1. Take the Six through to the Ten of Pentacles cards and continue your story from the previous section. Previously, you started at Five and worked back to the Ace; the reason for this is that there is no real "right order" when using mystical numbers. It shows that going back to "One" can sometimes be the most fulfilling journey.

2. Now, place the Ace in front of the Six, and start a new story. Write down key words for the cards in front of you, and as before write one or two sentences that describe a scenario where you won a million on the lottery. What happened next according to one-word interpretations of the cards?

THE SUIT OF SWORDS

KEYS

- Mind-set
- Thoughts
- Logic
- Ideals
- Illusion
- Mental struggles

MEANING

Associated with the astrological Air signs—Gemini, Libra, and Aquarius—the suit of Swords is about our rational and logical way of solving problems on a day-to-day basis. Yet, on closer inspection of the images, it seems that all these people look not only lonely, but rather tragic! This is because the mind isn't always our best friend. The mind is highly defensive, and fabricates inner conflicts and outer power plays, sometimes beneficial but often negative or even evil. There is a belief that if we reason with our emotions and rationalize away our desires, we will sort out our problems, but it is the mind that has (usually) created the problem in the first place. Swords also say, yes, we have a mind-set but we also have instincts and intuition; the logical left brain must also learn to work with the right side (intuition) and the wisdom of the heart.

Swords, therefore, can help us to "cut through" our illusions, and show us the real demons we need to face. If you draw a majority of Swords in any one layout, then you are very much living in your head at the moment—great for business or organizing the world, but not for the soul. It may be that you need to open yourself up to your inner voice, feelings, and real emotional needs.

MEET THE SWORDS COURT CARDS

WHAT YOU WILL NEED:

• The four Swords court cards
• A pen
• Paper or journal

WHAT YOU WILL EXPERIENCE:

• How your mind works

If the people on the numbered cards seem alone and tragic, the four court cards look like they've overcome their inner demons and are ready to face the world with shrewd thinking or swift action. There's a no-nonsense air about them.

1. Remove the Swords court cards from the deck and imagine you have invited these characters to a lavish dinner. Take one other card from the Major Arcana and place it facedown. This card represents yourself as the host, and the four court cards are guests sitting at the table in a line according to rank.

2. Now write down a few words to describe these people. Do you feel uncomfortable with them at your dinner table or happy to indulge in intellectual banter for an hour or so?

3. Based on their mind-set, what sort of after-dinner chat would they have? Write a short script for each one based on the Swords' energy. For example, the Knight might say, "I think you overcooked the chicken to the point of it being rubbery, but the Chardonnay was divine, must dash…"

4. Once you have written down your scripts, turn over your own card, and intuitively interpret what the card tells you about "your reaction" to these guests rather than what you personally think of them!

5. Now turn to the following pages to see how these Sword court cards can be interpreted and whether they fit your descriptions. Even if they don't, you're on the road to understanding that it's important not to stick with only one interpretation for a card, but open yourself up to associated ideas.

THE SWORDS COURT CARDS

The characters representing the Swords court cards brandish their swords and know what they want. They represent the power of the mind and how to use it.

PAGE OF SWORDS

KEYS

○— Objective thinking
○— Vigilance
○— Ready to be challenged
○— In the "know"
○— Youthful ideas
○— Mental dexterity

When you draw the Page of Swords, always remember that like all the other Pages, new ventures look promising, but something else is needed in order to maintain the pace. If you draw this card in the "you now" position, it is almost like a green light saying "go for it." It's time to get started on a new project or an idea, and to share that with others. With mental agility and anticipation, you will see beneficial results if you are vigilant of intellectual challenges to come. In the blockage position, stop deceiving yourself—you know all the answers.

KNIGHT OF SWORDS

KEYS

○— Frank
○— Incisive
○— Critical
○— Self-assured
○— Tactless
○— Impatient
○— Analytical
○— Powerful intellect

Like the other knights, our sword-brandishing cavalier represents extremes of the suit's energy—the most positive and negative qualities of the "mind." The Knight symbolizes all our vain assumptions of what we know or think we know. He represents our ability to criticize others, analyze a situation, get straight to the point, and wants everything explained in "black and white." In the "you now" position, use this energy positively to analyze a situation before making any decisions. The Knight can also manifest as a demanding, tactless lover or colleague. In the blockage position, you may be letting your head rule your heart, or someone in authority won't give you the chance to express your ideas.

QUEEN OF SWORDS
KEYS
- Direct
- Astute
- No-nonsense
- Up front and open
- Honest and quick-witted
- Clever mind

The Queen represents an acquired mind that is mature enough to understand all the facts. With intellectual ability and a strong character, she is ready to make a decision with realistic insight. Her hand is raised as if to make a swift decision. The Queen is discriminating and quick-witted. When she appears in a layout, someone who embodies these qualities will influence your life, or you yourself are about to reach a firm conclusion with total honesty. In the "you now" position, being direct and to the point

is the way forward. In a blockage position, the card suggests it's time to be less serious, or drop your judgmental attitudes.

KING OF SWORDS
KEYS
- Articulate
- Assertive
- Analytical
- Gets to grips with the situation
- High standards
- Intellectually adept

The King represents the most powerful energy of the suit, that of using the mind for problem-solving, cutting through mental confusion and challenging others with ideas. This energy is active, so when you draw this card in the "you now" position, you can handle your affairs, pit your wits against others, involve yourself in a debate to achieve success, or challenge others fairly with your plans. He can also represent someone influential in your life with high standards, who is assertive, and sure of him- or herself. As a blockage card, the King suggests you're too dogmatic and intolerant, or someone is intellectually trying to control you. The King is sure of himself, and his best armor are his wit and knowledge, so whenever you draw this card, use both!

THE SWORDS NUMBER CARDS

The Swords number cards all show people either in trouble or trying to get out of trouble. The problems are all ones they have created in their heads.

I	II	III	IV	V

SWORDS	SWORDS	SWORDS	SWORDS	SWORDS

ACE OF SWORDS
KEYS
- Clarity
- Facing facts
- Resolving a problem
- Realizing the way forward

The Ace of Swords heralds a time of great insight. It signifies a breakthrough where suddenly everything becomes clear, and the achievement of goals becomes viable. You have a new understanding of some issue that has been of concern. You can now get to the heart of the matter. As a "you now" card, you can achieve anything you desire.

TWO OF SWORDS
KEYS
- Blind to the truth
- Denial
- Blocking emotions
- Putting up barriers
- Being unavailable

The Two of Swords symbolizes one of our greatest problems: denial of feelings and not being honest enough to face the truth. Here, the Swords' illusions show that we are avoiding our feelings, hoping that it will all go away. If you draw this card in the "you now" position, think whether you are avoiding your feelings or someone else's; alternatively you may be cutting yourself off from someone else.

THREE OF SWORDS
KEYS
- Betrayal
- Broken heart
- A painful truth
- Separation
- Rejection

From the Two's denial of decision-making, the Three of Swords recognizes a choice has been made. You are now experiencing the consequences of that action. But the positive influence of the Three of Swords is to get to the heart of the difficult situation, and realize that in your loss or sorrow, there is a chance to move on to something better.

FOUR OF SWORDS
KEYS
- Repose
- Contemplation
- Taking a break
- Time to reevaluate
- Recharging your batteries

The knight is having a rest—he has put down his sword and is ready to take time out from the mental struggles of the past two cards. When you draw this card in the "you now" position, confrontation with others is not appropriate now—stand back, retreat, take a break from the struggle. Think things through and contemplate your situation. As a blockage card, constructive communication is needed, not retreating from the world.

FIVE OF SWORDS
KEYS
- Conquest
- Defeat
- Hollow victory
- Accepting limitations

There are many interpretations for this card. As a positive "you now" card, you have conquered and won a battle, despite the odds. It could represent a hollow victory, or accepting your limitations. As a blockage card, there is hostility or conflict in your life. As a future card, don't argue your cause every time someone has a different opinion, and you'll lead a more peaceful existence.

THE SWORDS NUMBER CARDS: PART ONE

1. Place the first five number cards face up on the table. Write down one interjection (choose an example from the list below or use your own) for each card, such as "the Three of Swords—ouch!"

Alas, Oops, Ouch, Phew, Shucks, Ugh, Oh!

2. Now, with each of the five words you chose, make up a sentence that will bring to life your character's exclamation. This can be fun or serious. For example, Three of Swords: "Ouch, that was the most painful truth I've ever experienced."

3. Keep the paper and the sentences for now, as you'll need them for the next exercise.

VI	VII	VIII	IX	X

SWORDS	SWORDS	SWORDS	SWORDS	SWORDS

SIX OF SWORDS

KEYS

○—► Recovery

○—► Travel

○—► New departure

○—► Leaving the past behind

○—► Moving out of troubled waters

The hooded figure on the boat represents sadness and loss. However, there is a positive aspect to this card as we can see the boatman is heading for calmer waters. This card indicates you are about to move from any sense of loss and despair to a calmer, happier state of mind. As a "you now" card, you may have been through some troubled times, but now you can start to live again and move forward. As a blockage card, you feel bogged down in problems and need to make an effort to move on.

SEVEN OF SWORDS

KEYS

○—► Deception

○—► Dishonesty

○—► Stealth

○—► Running from the truth

○—► Cheating

○—► Getting away with it

○—► Manipulative behavior

The word "deception" covers a host of personal issues and, depending on the other cards in the layout, will usually determine whether it's your own personal bending of the truth, self-deception, or dishonest behavior from others. Whatever the case, someone is "getting away" with something. In the "you now" position, are you really being honest with yourself? As a blockage card, a trickster, sneak, liar, or cheat is manipulating you.

EIGHT OF SWORDS

KEYS

○—► Self-sabotage

○—► Bound by your illusions

○—► Powerless

○—► Isolation

○—► Waiting to be rescued

The woman is bound and blindfolded, and doesn't seem to be trying very hard to escape. When you draw this card in the "you now" position, you might be hoping someone will come and save you, but no one can save us from ourselves. This card always indicates a trap, restriction, and an inability to shift—whether stuck in a bad job, a bad relationship, or a boring lifestyle. It's time to find a way out on your own—there is a way out between the swords if only the woman made an effort to free herself.

NINE OF SWORDS
KEYS
- Guilt
- Overwhelmed with worries
- Obsessive thinking
- Refusing to forgive

This card certainly looks like a nightmare. Can it get any bleaker? We've all had thoughts and worries that create fear and guilt in our mind, causing pain and emotional heartache. This card in the "you now" position indicates it's timely to look within for the source of your worries or obsession. Refocus and be honest about your vulnerability. On a positive note, the darkest hours are followed by the dawn.

TEN OF SWORDS
KEYS
- Culmination/enlightenment
- Turning point
- Feeling life is against you
- Betrayal

The Ten of Swords encapsulates the terrors of the mind of the past nine cards. Yet its alarming image holds positive qualities. If you get this as a "you now" card, you are ready to embark on a new journey. Even if everything seems bad, and you're depressed, the only way out is to get up and start again. This card can also reveal that someone you trust has betrayed you; you are shocked and angry. This card urges you to move on.

THE SWORDS NUMBER CARDS: PART TWO

1. Take your exclamation/interjection words and the cards Six to Ten of Swords. Study the cards carefully and take your five phrases from the previous exercise. Try to add a reason as to why you made these remarks by adding the word "because," and then matching them to one of the last five cards via their key words. For example: Three of Swords, "Ouch, finding out the truth was painful, because…(Eight of Swords) up until now, I've been bound by my illusions."

2. You should start to understand the "reasoning" nature of the mind and the Sword cards.

THE SUIT OF CUPS

KEYS
- Feelings
- Connection
- Sensitivity
- Love
- Passion

MEANING

The suit of Cups (also known as Chalices) is linked to the astrological Water signs—Cancer, Scorpio, and Pisces. These signs are associated with qualities that connect us to the outside world and other people, and how we perceive, attract, feel, and respond to that sense of "otherness."

The positive benefits of this suit give you a clear indication of most relationship issues, including love affairs, friendships, or familial relationships. Relationships are usually signified when you see a Cup card. When they turn up frequently in a layout, they signify that relating is a major issue for you right now.

A good way to understand our "feeling" world is to imagine the whole world of people feeling the same thing, from grief, or love, or passion, or desire, or loss. Feelings are universal; it affects all of us. However, if you fear emotions, you are shutting yourself out from understanding the world of the Cups. If you let yourself be touched by feeling, then you will find it easy to interpret these cards. Most of the numbered cards show people relating to the world, so think of the Cups as "relationship" cards.

MEET THE CUPS COURT CARDS

WHAT YOU WILL NEED:

• The four Cups court cards
• A pen
• Paper or a journal

WHAT YOU WILL EXPERIENCE:

• A sense of empathy

The Cups court cards reveal characters who understand human emotion and are naturally empathetic towards others.

QUEEN

CUPS

1. Take the four court cards and lay them face up in front of you. Carefully study the images. What might they be offering in their personal cup?

2. For each character, write down three ways that they "relate" to the world. How would you describe each card? What do they mean?

3. Finally, imagine each of the court cards as lovers. How would they show or tell the object of their affection that they were in love? For example, the Queen's body language looks so generous and kind that she might show her love by showering someone with affection.

4. Write a little script for each character, and then turn to the following pages to see the various general interpretations to help you form a wider understanding of these cards.

THE CUPS COURT CARDS

These court cards depict people who look as if they have experienced hard times and have now come to terms with themselves and can offer genuine love.

PAGE	KNIGHT	QUEEN	KING

CUPS	CUPS	CUPS	CUPS

PAGE OF CUPS

KEYS

- Sensitivity
- Inspired love
- Creative idea
- A lighthearted lover
- Forgiveness

Apart from appearing in your life as a young admirer or youthful lover, the Page of Cups also indicates that an inspirational idea has surfaced from the well of universal knowledge. The Page is also the kind of lover who may be immature or naïve in some way, but embodies innocent romance. In the "you now" position, your sensitivity is the key to your happiness. As a blockage card, are you being offered enough, or is someone offering you enough?

KNIGHT OF CUPS

KEYS

- Overflowing with emotion
- Idealization
- In love with love
- Temperamental
- Emotional rescue
- Gushing sentiments, but suspect intentions

The Knight of Cups represents extremes of the suit's energy. So on one level he is full of pure feeling, ready to lay down his life for you, on another he is so theatrical about life and his own feelings, that he is immune to anyone else's. This card also often turns up in a spread when we are not being honest about our feelings, or we just want to be rescued by a knight in shining armor. As a "you now" card, you may be idealizing a love affair, or are about to rush headlong into a crazy affair. The card can also represent the ideal lover, or someone who comes into your life full of charm and seductive ways. As a blockage card, are you in love with love rather than the real person?

QUEEN OF CUPS
KEYS
- Empathy
- Tenderness
- Unconditional love
- Compassionate
- Patient and kind
- Willing to help others

In the "you now" position, the Queen of Cups indicates you are full of understanding and tolerance for others, and it is a high priority in your life. This means you will attract people to you who are in need of your good nature and respect for others. In the future or outcome position, someone who embodies these qualities will come into your life to influence you, or you will develop great tenderness and compassion for others. As a blockage card, you may be too involved with someone else's problems to see your own.

KING OF CUPS
KEYS
- Emotional security
- Acceptance of one's limitations
- Stability
- Wisdom
- Generosity
- Acting rather than reacting

The King sits in the middle of a rough sea, revealing how secure his throne is while all around him, dolphins leap and ships flounder. The King knows that he can rely on himself and his calm approach to life. When you draw this card in the "you now" position, it reflects either your ability to make a wise choice based on your mature emotional attitude, or a stabilizing personality will enter your life for the better. As a blockage card, your feelings are being repressed either from self-sabotaging behavior or from a controlling person.

As an outcome card, you will be able to achieve all you want in the external world rather than reacting to others' expectations.

THE CUPS NUMBER CARDS

The numbered Cups cards show people relating to the outside world, whether alone or accompanied by others.

ACE OF CUPS
KEYS
- New love or romance
- Expressing love
- Desire for a deeper connection

The Aces always signify a new beginning. If you draw this as a "you now" card, a new connection is fuelling your emotional world. As a future or outcome card, it indicates some kind of gift is coming your way. As a blockage card, you are so enraptured by feelings that you can't see the wood for the trees.

TWO OF CUPS
KEYS
- Bonding
- Attraction
- Connection
- Reconciliation

If you are looking for a new romance, this is a card of instant attraction if drawn as a future card. As a "you now" card, you're sexually attractive, able to commit yourself and put the past behind you. As a blockage card, you're so wrapped up in your twosome that you're unable to retain your independence.

THREE OF CUPS
KEYS
- Friendship
- Celebration
- Team spirit
- Sharing good feelings

After the close intimacy of Two comes Three, where we have to open up to the world and share our joy. As a "you now" card, the Three of Cups simply tells you it's time to make new friends, celebrate, or get involved in beneficial teamwork.

As a blockage card, you're socializing so much you can't sort out your priorities.

FOUR OF CUPS
KEYS
- Introspection
- Self-absorbed
- Not seeing what's on offer
- Don't take life for granted

This card indicates that you are afraid to reach out and the isolation in your world is self-imposed. You may be only concerned with your own troubles and problems, neglecting the needs of others. In the "you now" position, your detachment from being part of the world is becoming an issue. So look up, and see the cup being offered to you, rather than bemoaning your fate.

FIVE OF CUPS
KEYS
- Loss
- Disappointment
- Regrets
- Time to let go of loss

This card appears to be negative—the figure is gazing intently only at the fallen cups, not noticing that there are two other upright ones. When we submerge ourselves in feelings of regret, loss, or even grief, we forget the positive side. This card tells you to accept the loss and pick up the remaining two cups filled with goodness for the future.

THE CUPS NUMBER CARDS: PART ONE

1. Take the Ace through to the Five of Cups, and lay them in a line before you.

2. Reflect upon the Five of Cups and recall any losses or regrets in your own life.

3. Examine the Four of Cups. Think, how did you react to the loss? Did you fall into the self-pity trap? Or were you able to move on?

4. Now look at the Three of Cups. Did you find new and positive things after the loss?

5. Now reflect on the Two of Cups. Did you look for a new bond, or renew a bond that had been lost? Do you relate easily to the outside world?

6. Now take the Ace, which represents pure, untainted love. How do you relate to romance? How do you relate to relating?

SIX OF CUPS
KEYS
- Playful innocence
- Nostalgia
- Goodwill to all
- Sharing

In the "you now" position, fond memories will show you the way forward. It is time to enjoy and share your life with others; by giving out goodness, it will come back tenfold. As a future or outcome card, someone from the past may return, but only for positive benefits. As a blockage card, you're being too naive about a relationship.

SEVEN OF CUPS
KEYS
- Wishful thinking
- High expectations
- Self-indulgence
- Too many options

The bizarre items rising from the seven cups represent all those things we desire in life. When you draw this card in the "you now" position, there are three possible interpretations. One, that you are living under some kind of illusion about love; two, indulging in all kinds of excesses in your relationship to the world; and three, you have so many choices to make, you are putting off taking the plunge.

EIGHT OF CUPS
KEYS
- Moving on
- Changing direction
- Walking away from the past
- Deeper meaning in life

The Eight of Cups signifies a time of change that comes from within. There is an inner feeling that things have to shift, evolve, and move on. It's time to restore inner balance and emotional harmony. As a blockage card, it is the very fear of moving on that is creating obstacles for you.

NINE OF CUPS

KEYS

- Feeling blessed
- Wishes fulfilled
- Satisfaction
- Enjoying the good life

The Nine of Cups reminds us that we can find new ways to be fulfilled. In the "you now" position, it's time to enjoy yourself and be you. As a future card the chances are "stacked" in your favor and a current wish or dream will come true. As a blockage card, you're so sure of yourself, you won't listen to anyone else's viewpoint.

TEN OF CUPS

KEYS

- Joy
- Peace
- Harmony
- Promise of more to come
- Emotional fulfillment

In the "you now" position, this card signifies positive times and that the joy you seek is within reach. As a future card, you can soon welcome harmony and emotional contentment into your life. As a blockage card, you are idealizing the perfect relationship, and no one can live up to that image.

THE CUPS NUMBER CARDS: PART TWO

1. Lay the Six to Ten of Cups cards in front of you.

2. Study the Six of Cups—when deeply in love we are like children, naive and untouched by outside influences. Do you disappear from the world when you're in love, or do you play in front of an audience and show your happiness?

3. The Seven suggests your ideals are under challenge. Does love live up to your ideals?

4. The Eight indicates moving on. Have you ever left someone? What did it feel like?

5. The Nine of Cups represents feeling fulfilled, blessed, and content with life. Have you experienced this? If so, what did it feel like? If not, what can you do about it?

6. Reflect on the Ten of Cups. Are our ideals achievable? What would it feel like to be so happy?

MINOR ARCANA EXERCISE

WHAT YOU WILL NEED:

- A candle (to symbolize Fire)
- A piece of paper and pen (to symbolize Air)
- A piece of carnelian or amber (to symbolize Earth)
- A pearl, shell, or piece of mother-of-pearl (to symbolize Water)

WHAT YOU WILL EXPERIENCE:

- A boost to your interpretative powers

This exercise blends the cards from all the suits to help develop your interpretative and intuitive powers.

Rather than sticking to one suit, you're going to mix and match the cards from the Minor Arcana and see what you can interpret by just using the basic principle of suit, number, and/or status of court card.

You'll also see patterns developing and recognize them not just by the image but by the key symbols of each suit.

1. Cut the Minor Arcana into its four suits; shuffle each suit and cut once. Place the four stacks facedown in the following order: the Pentacles to the north (Earth), Wands to the south (Fire), Swords to the east (Air), and Cups to the west (Water).

2. Next, place a candle beside the suit of Wands, the paper and pen beside the suit of Swords, the carnelian beside the suit of Pentacles, and the pearl or shell beside the suit of Cups. These represent the energies of the four elements.

3. Close your eyes and relax by counting down slowly from twenty to one.

4. Now open your eyes and repeat the following charm three times to align yourself to the four elements:

By powers of Fire and Water too
Of Earth and Air and tarot true
I am of Universal Light
To know the Truth, that is my right.

5. Take one card from the top of each stack starting with north and go in a clockwise direction.

6. Place the four cards face up on the table in a straight line in front of you.

7. Without thinking about what the images on the cards depict, look straight away to the numbers and the suit. Take a word that comes to you which you immediately associate with the number, and a word that comes to you immediately which you associate with the suits. Write these down on your sheet of paper.

FOR EXAMPLE: I have chosen the Four of Pentacles, the Ten of Swords, the Six of Wands, and the King of Cups. My associated words, off the top of my head:

Four—motivation; Pentacles—practical; Ten—achievement; Swords—logical; Six—harmonious; Wands—spirited; King—powerful; Cups —feelings.

What message is being sent by these words? Get cracking!

Now do the same thing yourself, without looking up any interpretations for the Minor Arcana. You too will "see" a message written in the cards without having to resort to the traditional meanings.

You can continue drawing cards from stacks in this way until you feel you've done enough for one session. Don't overdo it, or you'll lose that "flash" of insight that comes best when we're fresh, calm, and not under pressure to "perform."

PENTACLES

SWORDS

WANDS

CUPS

CHAPTER FOUR

THE KEY
to
INTERPRETING SPREADS

○━➤ Spreads align us to the energy of the Universe

○━➤ The first card drawn is the most potent

○━➤ Three-card readings help you develop your skills quickly

○━➤ The blockage card helps identify negative energy

INTRODUCTION TO SPREADS

I've often been asked why we lay out the cards in spreads. Why not just take random cards and just place them down in a long line and read them one after another like pages of a book? As we all know, we live in a world of beginnings and endings, a world fixated on measurement and chronological order. But the tarot doesn't conform to this kind of perception.

It doesn't start at A and end at Z. Take the Major Arcana—when you get to the World, there is the Fool to consider again. He is not "unnumbered" for nothing, and he is the link that takes us full circle to the beginning.

There are simple spreads made of just three or four cards in a "line;" they are included here to help you start out. Spreads with some form of symbolic structure—for example, the pentagram spread or the mystic seven spread—take us deeper into sacred geometry, aligning us to the harmonic energies of the Universe. Spreads are symbolic patterns as well as a display of symbolic moments. Putting these together isn't a jigsaw; it's simply a way of perceiving what is in front of you as a whole. By piecing together the symbols in a story, we can arrive at a simple truth. But eventually, you'll just "know" what a spread of seven cards means.

The rest of this chapter includes a wide range of spreads to get you going. But do work through them chronologically, because you will find it easier to build up to the more complicated spreads. Start with the quick and easy spreads to get you going. These spreads are also useful for resolving simple issues, or for self-knowledge on a daily basis. They are great for being creative and intuitive about the meanings of the cards, rather than boring yourself by always using the same interpretation from this book, or any other for that matter.

We're also going to look at relationship spreads, which tell you about the dynamics of relationships. These are followed by more advanced spreads, where the structure and layout resonate to sacred geometry and other universal or astrological patterns. These spreads are designed to delve into the archetypal nature of the Universe. Although I have named them "destiny" spreads, they are really revelations in the sense of discovering what you really want for the future and what influences you can expect to help or hinder you.

The art of interpreting the spreads is to remember that they are a reflection of you at the moment you chose the cards.

If you disassociate yourself totally from the cards, you may have greater objectivity reading them but less ability to engage with your deeper needs and desires. So the flow or bridge between objectivity and "intuition" is what the tarot is; this is what the tarot allows you to experience, the harmony between the awareness of your objective self and your subjective self.

You can be creative with your layouts, but when you first start use the simplest spreads.

UNDERSTANDING WHAT THE SPREADS SYMBOLIZE

This exercise will enable you to understand the symbolic nature of spreads, the placement of the cards, and why the symbolic patterns of spreads can give you deeper insights behind the nature of the cards.

WHAT YOU WILL NEED:
• Five cards (any will do, you're not going to look at the images)
• Pen and paper

WHAT YOU WILL EXPERIENCE:
• Being at one with a spread

We're going to take the pentagram spread, because we've been using this shape in various ways throughout the book so far.

The pentagram is a geometrical shape made up of a five-pointed star (with the fifth point pointing upwards; see diagram). It has been used as a sign of completion and harmony in occult and mystical circles.

Fascinatingly, the orbit of the planet Venus forms an irregularly shaped pentagram every six or so years, and the musical harmonic of five is also associated with Venus. We know that five corresponds to creativity and Venus to the qualities of charisma. In other words, before you

even begin to "read" the cards, you are engaging in the symbolism of "five." If each point of the star is also associated with an astrological element and the spirit of wholeness as the quintessential element, then each point of that star brings a deeper layer of understanding to the card itself.

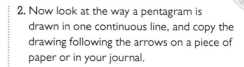

1. Place five cards facedown on the table in the shape of the pentagram. Look at the diagram here, and you'll see that each card corresponds to a "direction," an astrological element, and a keyword.

> N = Spirit
> NE = Earth, Manifestation
> SE = Air, Reflection
> SW = Fire, Action
> NW = Water, Intuition

2. Now look at the way a pentagram is drawn in one continuous line, and copy the drawing following the arrows on a piece of paper or in your journal.

3. So we start with Spirit, then take an angled line down to the SE point and Air, followed by an angle back up to the NW point, and Water, then directly across to the NE to Earth, then an angle back down to Fire at the SW point, finishing with a line back up to the N and Spirit again.

   This is the correct format for laying out the pentagram spread. By laying the cards down in the order shown, you are creating a "true pentagram" and the cards will reveal the truth of your physical engagement in the geometry itself. A beautiful moment when you read the cards and know you are part of that spread, not just an onlooker!

4. Now take up the cards, and place them back down in the order of the drawn lines. Do you feel or intuit any difference?

THE POSITIONS

Now we come to another less subtle part of reading spreads, but these are incredibly useful when you're a beginner. These are the main positions that we talked about briefly in Chapter One, and they are referred to throughout the interpretations of the cards in both the Major Arcana and Minor Arcana chapters. These positions are important because they allow you to focus on specific cards and their relationship to the question or type of spread you're working with.

Some cards are easy to interpret because they have a very obvious meaning, like the Three of Cups, which suggests "having fun" or enjoying oneself.

THE "YOU NOW" CARD

Most spreads, as mentioned before, have a focus card. Usually, this is the first card chosen because it is your first immediate engagement with the Universe and what it's "trying to tell you." So I've often called this card the "you now" card. Instantly, you can relate to this card and realize that this is a reflection of you and no one else. It is likely that this will become the real focus card, and it is this placement that is therefore hugely important.

However, there are times when the "you now" card may turn out to be a Minor Arcana with a rather easy or simple symbolic resonance, rather than a juicy Major Arcana card with its deeper layers of meaning. For example, say you chose as your first card—the Three of Cups with three ladies dancing. You may, on one level, like this because it suggests you're having a good time, or you might wonder whether it can really help you in any way. If that latter is the case, look at the spread as a whole and see if any other card "speaks" to you or stands out from the others. It is likely that this card is the focus card, and its placement is therefore hugely important.

THE "BLOCKAGE" CARD

The "blockage" card is simply a useful card to replace the reversed card usage, which I believe is not necessary when first learning the tarot. The blockage card identifies the things in your life that are holding you back, stopping you from making your choices, or negative influences you need to attend to.

THE "OUTCOME" OR "FUTURE" CARD

The "outcome" or "future" card is exactly what it says. Here, you are being given the result of all the other cards in the spread, but it doesn't mean this is the finite answer! Remember the tarot has no ending nor beginning, and so, say, if you had the "Hanged Man" as your outcome card, it wouldn't mean that you would spend the rest of your life in eternal limbo, having to see things from another angle. It all depends on the length of time we determine for events to unfold.

I would recommend that most simple spreads look only to the next few days or week at the most; more complex spreads for a few weeks to a month. So when you ask a question for an open reading, for example, you must decide for what kind of period in the future you are expecting results before doing the reading.

XII

THE HANGED MAN

The "outcome" card is not about a fixed future, it just describes another step on your life journey.

LAYING OUT THE CARDS

Here is an exercise for laying out a spread. There are no rules about how you do it, but it's useful to follow these guidelines so that you are always prepared and have a chance to relax and open yourself to the energy of the cards.

WHAT YOU WILL NEED:
- Your tarot deck
- Your tarot journal or piece of paper
- A pen
- A white candle
- Favorite incense

WHAT YOU WILL EXPERIENCE:
- Seeing how spreads are symbolic on many levels

1. Find a quiet, comfortable environment so you can focus and also begin to connect to your intuitive voice. Light the candle and incense, and make sure you have space in front of you to lay out the cards.

2. Place your tarot journal (or the pen and paper) beside you to make notes as you go along. Before you begin, write down your question or issue so that it's clear in your head. Sometimes it's easy to twist the original question to fit the response and interpretation of the cards!

3. Shuffle the cards in one of the recommended ways as described in Chapter One. As you shuffle, focus on the question or issue. For this exercise, we are going to use seven cards in a spread, but don't worry—you're not going to interpret this spread but merely use it as a way of understanding the structure and process of tarot work. For this exercise and for all the other spreads in this book, draw the relevant number of cards one by one after your chosen shuffling system (see page 24). Lay each card facedown in the order and position shown in the spread diagram.

4. Once you have laid the cards facedown, you can turn them up one by one. If any of the cards are reversed, for now, as a beginner, ignore this and simply turn them the right way up.

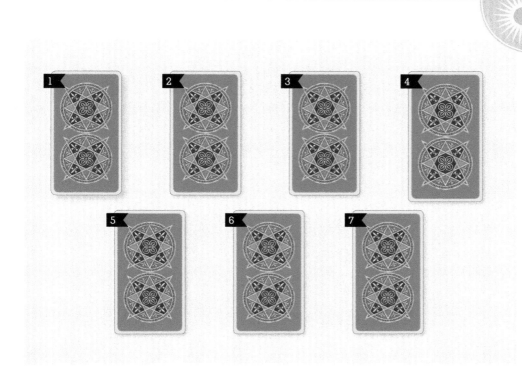

5. Look at each of the cards and see if you can find any repeat patterns of imagery, suits, or numbers; make notes in your journal as you go along.

6. Write down one keyword for each card according to the book, along with any intuitive flashes you have.

7. Once you have completed this exercise, write down the following:

○━➤ When I lay out the structure of the spread, this is represented by Pentacles.

○━➤ My interpretation of the spread is symbolized by the joint energy of Swords and Wands.

○━➤ My response to the interpretation is represented by Cups.

This is to remind you that when you engage in the language of the tarot, it works on many symbolic layers, not just to give answers to questions.

HOW TO INTERPRET THREE CARDS

To get you going, let's start with three-card readings. Three is a good number because it can be easily broken down into "past, present, future," or "you now, you then, you in the future," and so on. In fact, three cards can give you answers to a multitude of questions, and if you use a three-card spread on a daily basis, it also helps develop your interpretation skills.

There are no rules. As I've said before, each person will read the cards differently (according to their own psychological makeup) even if they align to the traditional interpretations. It takes practice, openness, and a willingness to learn and develop your skill. After that, the language of symbols will become as simple as the language you speak every day. Soon, you will be able to read the cards as if you were reading a book.

The secret of interpreting more than one card at a time is to become a storyteller who recounts the tale aloud, as if you had an audience.

SIMPLE THREE-CARD SPREAD

Practice with this easy spread first. In the example shown below, the middle card represents your present situation or "you now;" the second card represents future action; and the third card shows the outcome.

1. Shuffle and choose three cards, and lay them out in the order below, face up.

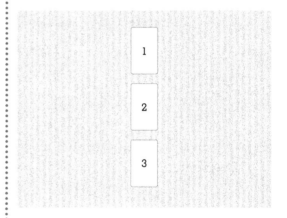

LET'S SAY YOUR QUESTION IS:
How do I find new romance?

In this example, the first card drawn in the "you now" position is the Hierophant; the second card, the Two of Wands, and the third card, Strength.

V

HIEROPHANT

II

WANDS

VIII

STRENGTH

2. Look at each card individually and its associated placement in relation to the question.

The Hierophant is generally interpreted as "conventional" and "doing what's expected." How do you relate this to the "you now" position and romance? What does this sound like to you? Perhaps one example interpretation would be, "I am too conventional about how I find romance, which isn't helping to meet someone new."

The second card, the Two of Wands, is simply interpreted as "showing you mean business." As a future action card related to the question, it could be interpreted as "maybe I have to assert myself, and go out there and find romance, rather than assume it will come to me."

The third card represents the short-term outcome of the question. Strength indicates "taking control of your life," suggesting that in the future, romance will come to you if you are more self-assured and take responsibility for your actions.

The spreads on the following pages are designed to take you step by step toward more complex readings. Starting with three-card spreads, I have provided example readings to help you, and as ever, look at the tarot as a chance to know yourself better. Enjoy these exercises!

THREE CARDS FOR THE DAY

Apart from drawing a card every day to see what kind of day you can expect, these two spreads will enable you to get to know the cards and the range of combinations available. These spreads will not only exercise your interpretative skills, but also your ability to be objective because you will have to ask yourself some questions and give yourself some truthful answers!

TASKS FOR THE DAY

LAYING THE CARDS

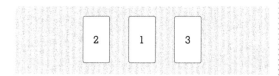

1. What is most important today?
2. What needs attention?
3. What do I watch out for?

Lay the cards out as above.
Here are the questions you need to ask yourself for each of the cards.

CARD ONE: This card is important for me today. When I interpret it, can I connect to this as important? Or do I find it hard to engage in its meaning/quality?
CARD TWO: I need to act on or attend to this today, but does it/will it feel threatening or satisfying to do so?
CARD THREE: The things I must watch out for can be emotional reactions, outside influences or new desires. Do I resent, fear, or embrace the findings of this card?

EXAMPLE READING

1. **Seven of Pentacles:** A day when you can evaluate and assess the fruits of your labor.
2. **King of Swords:** Contact someone articulate and assertive for your benefit, or act on intellectual knowledge rather than gut instinct.
3. **Nine of Pentacles:** Be careful of assuming you've achieved your best, there is more to come.

ENERGY OF THE DAY

LAYING THE CARDS

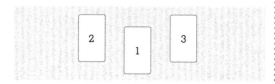

1. The energy of your day
2. Interferences
3. Positive results

Here are the interactive questions you need to ask once you've drawn the cards.

1. Do you resist or welcome this energy?
2. Does this feel threatening, or is it actually a welcome interference?
3. The results may not be what you want, but they might be what you need. Do you know the difference?

EXAMPLE READING

1. **Four of Wands:** The energy around you is exuberant and easy.
2. **Seven of Cups:** The interference is your own wishful thinking, or a dreamy character.
3. **The Fool:** Positive energy—realization that you can go your own way.

CUPS

WANDS

THE FOOL

BEST AND WORST

This is different from the others because you consciously have to choose two cards and only choose one card at random. First, you must choose the card you like the most and second, the card you don't like even if you're not sure why.

Take the deck and really take your time to look through the cards. You may already have them decided in your mind, but if one seems to leap out at you, put it to one side until you have finished looking through. Obviously, if you have to make a choice between two or three "favorites," then so much the better to stretch your decision-making ability!

You can do this spread every few days, as you may well find over time that you change your mind about the cards you like and the cards you loathe.

LAYING THE CARDS

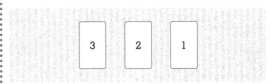

1. Best card
2. Learning card
3. Worst card

Lay out the best and worst cards in the positions shown in the diagram (1 and 3). Shuffle the rest of the deck as normal. Now draw one card at random and lay it facedown without looking (position 2).

Look up the interpretations for the best and worst cards. Think about what they mean for you, and why you chose them. Why did you like one and loathe the other? Write your thoughts down before you continue.

- Is the card you like representative of a quality, person, or experience?
- Is the card you dislike particularly significant? Are you blocking out these energies from your life, or projecting them onto others?
- Are you experiencing any of these qualities? Are you being objective?

Finally, turn over the middle card and discover what you need to learn right now.

EXAMPLE READING

1. **Queen of Cups:** I like this card best because the Queen represents all that I would like to be— compassionate, aware, tenderhearted.

2. **Death:** This card is the worst because it's a bit scary, and it represents change, which I can't bear.

3. **Seven of Swords:** This card suggests that I need to learn to not run away from the truth; that I do have the Queen of Cups qualities if I look within. I must also accept that change brings positive benefits.

SWORDS

DEATH

CUPS

RESOLVING AN ISSUE

This is a simple three-card spread for helping to resolve some kind of issue or problem—the kind that crops up on a day-to-day basis. We all have personal issues, and sometimes we are not sure what to do about them. Who do I turn to? Am I being selfish or stupid? Overreacting? Running from the truth? Even just answering these questions can pose enormous problems.

You may have a good awareness of what needs fixing. It could be a simple problem such as lack of communication with your partner, a problem at work, or the fear of commitment. Whatever the case, the first card focuses on the root cause of the problem; the second card shows what needs to be done to resolve the problem and how to deal with it; and third card suggests the outcome.

LAYING THE CARDS

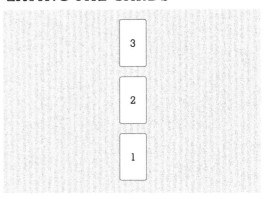

1. **Focus on the cause**
2. **What shall I do?**
3. **The outcome**

When you try this out for yourself, note if there is more than one Major Arcana card in the layout. If there are two or even three, then the chances are you're in need of a major change of perception; the Universe is trying to tell you to start making things happen in your life, rather than denying responsibility for your "fate." Ask yourself the following questions after you've interpreted the cards:

- Is this really such a big issue after all?
- Why have I become so indecisive/ uncertain/angry/confused?
- Do the cards, in relation to my problem, tell me the truth of the matter?

3 VII

THE CHARIOT

2 KING

WANDS

1 XVIII

THE MOON

EXAMPLE READING

THE PROBLEM: I can't make up my mind—should I take up a totally new career or not? I want to do it because it's a new challenge and I'm bored, but I fear leaving what I know and what I'm used to.

1. **The Moon:** I feel indecisive because I am uncomfortable about letting go, and I will be vulnerable in a new place.
2. **King of Wands:** Sticking to what I know is the easy option, but I have to show myself I can move on.
3. **The Chariot:** If I take up the new career, I will succeed.

BLOCKAGE

This is an easy spread to introduce you to the "blockage position." Often, when we are seeking answers to life's many questions, there always seems to be something that holds us back—something that feels like a negative influence or an obstacle. The blockage card enables us to identify what that "obstacle" may be, and most often, these blockages are actually all in our head. The first card describes "you now" and in this case, the attitude you currently have to what you truly want to let go of or drop. The second card is what is stopping you, the "blockage card;" and the third card is what action you must take to resolve the problem.

LAYING THE CARDS

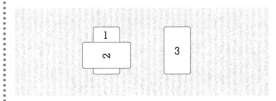

1. **You now**
2. **What is stopping me?**
3. **Action to take**

Before choosing the cards, think about what, or who, you want to move on from. You may want to be released from painful memories; an ex who you just can't get out of your mind, or a current date who is just too boring for words! Whatever it is, concentrate on the issue while you shuffle the cards, and keep focused on the issue in your mind while you interpret according to the positions.

EXAMPLE READING

1. **The Emperor:** You're feeling ready to tackle your problem and start to take control of your life again.
2. **Five of Swords:** What's stopping you from letting go of the past are the mind games you've got yourself into, which are in fact controlling you rather than you controlling your mind!
3. **Eight of Wands:** Get your priorities sorted out, and take swift action to make it clear what your intentions are.

Practice using blockage spreads as much as you can, even as "open readings." This allows you to look at the cards on a daily basis and to see what is currently going on. What is a blockage or problem? How can it be resolved?

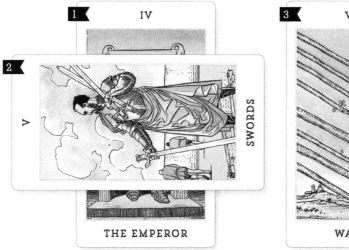
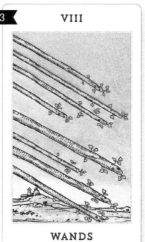

MYSTICAL THREE

To finish our exercises with three cards, try this spread to simply sum up the past, present, and future. This can be used to pin down what it is in your life that is important or needs attention. Sometimes when we reach for the tarot, we aren't even sure what we want or need to know. But this spread uses the mystical approach to tarot, in that you are going to count seven cards down into one of three stacks of the deck each time you draw a card. Seven is the mystical number associated with the harmony of the Universe. Three times (the three cards) seven (the number of cards you must count each time) equals twenty-one, and two and one makes our mystical three!

LAYING THE CARDS

For this spread you will also need three white candles to reinforce the mystical combination of the mystic three.

Light the candles before you begin. Take the deck of cards, shuffle, and cut into three stacks. Place each stack facedown on the table in a row. Now, take the first stack and with your finger count down from the top of the deck to the seventh card. Remove it without looking at it, and place it facedown at "position one." Do the same with the second stack, and place the seventh card in position two, and finally the last seventh card from the third stack in position three.

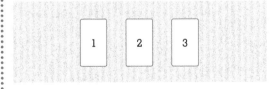

When you have finished, turn the card in position one over. This represents the recent past.

Before turning over the other cards, think what it means to you in relation to the past. Does it stir any ideas, memories, or gut feelings? Next, turn over the second card—this represents the present. What do you associate this card with? Does it have a negative energy or a positive one? Finally, turn over the last card, which represents the near future—the next twenty-four hours or so. What can you envisage this means to you in relation to the present, to now, this day?

Gaze into the candle flames and focus on these three energies or qualities represented by the cards. You can, of course, look to the meanings in this book as a guide, but more importantly, it's your connection to the Universe and your mystical powers that will be working with the tarot images, so let the feelings and intuition flow.

EXAMPLE READING

1. THE RECENT PAST:

The Chariot: I was motivated and challenged, and I was ready to win at all costs.

2. THE PRESENT:

Eight of Pentacles: I'm dedicated to current responsibilities, is this enough? (There is a doubt here—is this a positive or negative influence?)

3. THE NEAR FUTURE:

The Star: It will shortly be time to reveal my talents, be inspired into action, and show that I have more to offer. (The querent knows deep down that s/he needs to fulfill the energies of the past in the future.)

THE CHARIOT

PENTACLES

THE STAR

PRIORITIES

The two spreads on these pages will help you to understand how a three-card spread evolves into a five-card spread. The first spread simply reveals three major priorities you need to attend to in your life concerning love, career, and self-development. The second spread uses the first "you now" card as the main priority, followed by cards that reveal influences and, of course, the "blockage" card.

SPREAD ONE

LAYING THE CARDS

This little spread targets exactly what you need to attend to in each area of your life. Draw each card and place facedown. Don't turn up the next card you read until you have thoroughly understood the meaning of each card and its relationship to the position.

1. Love
2. Career
3. Self-development

1. **LOVE:**
   The Hermit: I need to seriously contemplate what love means to me.
2. **CAREER:**
   Two of Wands: I am ready to take a new direction, risk, or explore new horizons.
3. **SELF-DEVELOPMENT:**
   Ten of Pentacles: To be able to achieve all this, financial stability and inner security are important to me.

THE HERMIT

WANDS

PENTACLES

SPREAD TWO

LAYING THE CARDS

1. My priority right now
2. What is blocking me
3. The things I need to change
4. Helpful outside influences
5. The outcome

EXAMPLE READING

After you have shuffled the cards, draw the cards at random as usual, and place face up as you create the spread.

1. **The High Priestess:** My priority right now is to trust my intuition and really attend to my secret desire. (Ask yourself what that is.)
2. **Two of Pentacles:** I can't focus and I keep playing around with too many ideas in my mind rather than listening to my heart.
3. **Nine of Pentacles:** What needs to change is my sense of independence and the need to be more self-reliant.

4. **The Six of Wands:** Helpful outside influences are people who know how to be at the top of their profession.
5. **Queen of Swords:** The outcome is being more aware of my motives and my need to be seen as direct and to the point.

MY SECRETS

Taking things a little further, you are now going to use seven cards to further develop your skills. As with any spread, absolute honesty and self-awareness needed when you interpret the cards. But this spread calls for you to really look at the interpretations in an objective way.

LAYING THE CARDS

Lay the cards out one by one as shown in the diagram, and turn the cards facedown until it's time to interpret each card. This makes you focus on one card at a time rather than looking at seven cards all at once. Reading cards in combination will come a little later in the exercises.

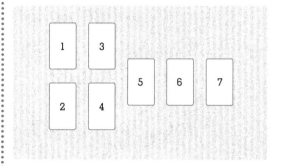

1. What is my secret desire?
2. What is my secret hate?
3. What is my secret challenge?
4. What is my secret need?
5. What is my secret test?
6. What is my secret motivation?
7. What can I accomplish?

1. **The Lovers:** My secret desire is to have an affair/fall in love/find commitment.
2. **Temperance:** My secret hate is being so compromising and nice to everyone.
3. **Four of Pentacles:** My secret challenge is to stop being so manipulated and start creating respect and order in my world.
4. **Death:** My secret need is to change my life completely, close one door and open another.
5. **Knight of Swords:** My secret test is to not let my heart rule my head.
6. **Ten of Cups:** My secret motivation is to have a stable and happy emotional life.
7. **King of Wands:** To meet a strong, charismatic character who will inspire me to live life as I secretly want to.

As you can see, this example aligns the cards to the "focus card"—the first card chosen. Even though some of the cards could be interpreted differently, if they are always related to the first card and the theme of the spread, you will create a story, rather than a muddled string of notes and not a harmonious chord.

THE LOVERS

PENTACLES

TEMPERANCE

DEATH

SWORDS

CUPS

WANDS

WHO AM I?

This is another seven-card spread that asks you to explore yourself a little deeper. These spreads are essential exercises for developing not only your personal objectivity, but for preparing you for the slightly longer spreads to come later. Once you can honestly look within, and learn a little about yourself (whether you believe in the mirror image you see before you or not), you will then be ready to read for other people. It's easy to project your own "ulterior motives" onto the reading, or what you would like to happen to or for your friend.

LAYING THE CARDS

Shuffle as usual then choose one card at a time. Lay out the cards facedown in this order, and turn them up one by one to clarify each card in turn.

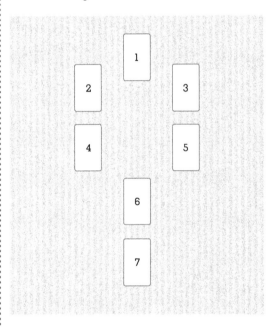

1. This is who I am right now
2. This is what I don't know about myself
3. This is what I need to relinquish
4. This is what I need to develop
5. My current quest
6. Outside positive influences
7. Where it will lead

1. **Queen of Wands:** I'm a fairly attractive, self-assured, and optimistic character.
2. **The Moon:** I did not realize I have an intuitive side that will enable me to tap into another way of looking at life.
3. **King of Swords:** I need to relinquish my logical, right-brained attitude.
4. **Three of Cups:** I need to get together with others, have more fun, or be more of a team player.
5. **Ace of Swords:** My current quest is to show I mean business in my career/work.
6. **Justice:** To help me on my quest, listen to good advice, don't ignore fair opinions.
7. **The Magician:** This will lead me to following the right direction and grounding my future aspirations.

Again, by aligning the focus card (the "you now" first card) with the rest of the cards and the theme of the spread, the interpretations create a story, so whether you tell it yourself aloud or in your head, you're building the words and structuring your external world from internal and universal truths.

GOALS AND OBJECTIVES

Sometimes we do spreads to motivate us, to make us reach for the phone or take the plunge when we're feeling fearful, weak, or indecisive. This spread will give you the confidence to follow your goals or aspirations. You can also use it if you're not sure what direction to take, or if you're uncertain whether you've made a good choice and whether you should stick to it!

LAYING THE CARDS

Lay out the cards as shown in the diagram, and this time, turn them all face up as you put them down in their position. Now you can start to see links, themes, and maybe even intuit what the whole spread is saying to you by the time you've laid down the seven cards. Remember that the focus card, the first card, is the power behind the rest of the cards.

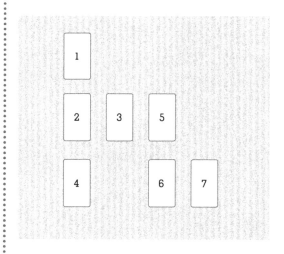

1. Current objective
2. Talent or skill
3. Lack
4. Beneficial influence
5. Potential
6. The promise of progress
7. The outcome

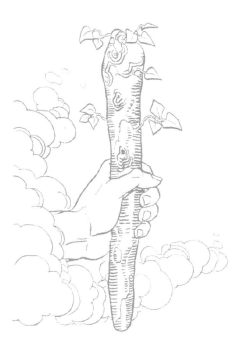

1. **The Sun:** I want to shine like the sun, have fun, and enjoy being in the spotlight.
2. **Ace of Wands:** My talent is my creative vision and original ideas.
3. **The Empress:** However, I lack the practical skills to take it any further.
4. **The Chariot:** Someone motivated and wise will help me out.
5. **Six of Pentacles:** I must look at what I can learn and gain from this.
6. **Nine of Cups:** I must realize that if I truly believe in my goal, it will come true.
7. **King of Pentacles:** I can make a success out of any venture if I put my mind to it.

Again, the more you relate the card to the question/issue and the theme of the layout, the easier it is to interpret.

THE SUN

WANDS

THE EMPRESS

PENTACLES

THE CHARIOT

CUPS

PENTACLES

PENTAGRAM DECISION-MAKER

This spread is designed to help you make a decision. So you first need to know what you're making a decision about—details are important. Even write it down on a piece of paper or in your journal first, so you don't go off on a tangent.

As you can see from the diagram, there are in fact six cards to interpret. The five points of the pentagram symbolize the energies of each of the tarot suits, with the Major Arcana represented by the topmost point. At the center, or core, of the pentagram, is the answer to the outcome of making the decision from the deep well of knowledge of the Universe.

LAYING THE CARDS

As you lay the cards out slowly in the order shown, imagine you are drawing a pentagram in your mind so that you can connect more deeply to this ancient symbol.

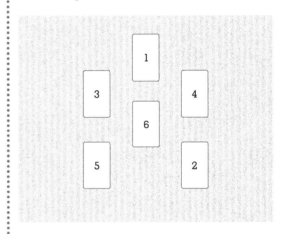

1. You now
2. Focus
3. Difficult influences
4. Beneficial influences
5. Unexpected insight
6. The decision

1. **Ace of Swords:** I am ready to be objective and make a good decision based on logic.
2. **The High Priestess:** I need to focus on the power of my intuition too.
3. **Three of Pentacles:** Others may not have my best interests at heart.
4. **Nine of Pentacles:** I must stick to my personal beliefs to help me arrive at a decision.
5. **The Tower:** A sudden change of attitude will steer me on the right course.

6. **The World:** The decision rests on whether I want a new voyage of discovery—am I willing to embark on this journey? (If, for example, the answer to this question is yes, make the decision and stick to it. If the answer is "no, I'm not ready," then do this spread again in a few days.)

The whole point of this spread is to develop your ability to make conscious choices for yourself, not to get the tarot to do it for you.

EXAMINING A RELATIONSHIP

Most of us turn to the tarot cards looking for answers to questions about our relationships. We may have just met someone, fallen in love, or we may be waiting for the first date. We may have just split up with someone, are feeling betrayed, or have got ourselves into a love triangle. Whatever the case, these relationship spreads offer a start for understanding how you can look at relationships objectively. The tarot will mirror your relationships, just as it will mirror you.

This spread reveals the dynamics of your relationship with someone. It can help you to see what the plus and minus points of it are, rather than looking at you and your partner as individuals. In fact, you are looking at the relationship itself as a separate entity. When you read this spread, pay attention to your own attitude or thoughts and the way you relate to the relationship as it is right now. Treat the relationship as a third party, with you as an onlooker.

LAYING THE CARDS

For this spread use only the Major Arcana for an in-depth interpretation.

It is now time to look at the cards as a whole, as well as individually. So as you lay them out, turn each card face up and imagine the spread is a painting on the wall. Before you begin to interpret each card, think about what the whole picture says to you. Is it a dance? Is it a mess? Is it a work of art? Is it delicate? Heavy-handed? Filled with negative or positive images (your projections)?

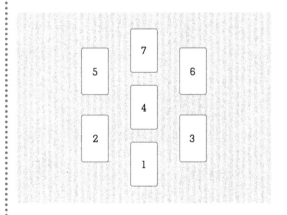

1. Its outward energy
2. Its hidden energy
3. Its strength
4. Its weakness
5. Its reality
6. Its passion
7. Its key to the future

EXAMPLE READING

1. **The Sun:** The relationship's energy is playful and creative.

2. **The Moon:** Behind the scenes, there are deeper feelings at work.

3. **The Fool:** Its strength is that it stays alive and forward thinking.

4. **The Chariot:** Its weakness is the underlying power play going on.

5. **Temperance:** The reality is it needs to find balance.

6. **The World:** Its passion is to live life to the full.

7. **The Empress:** Its key to the future is to come down to earth.

III

THE EMPRESS

XIV · 5

TEMPERANCE

VII · 4

THE CHARIOT

XXI · 6

THE WORLD

XVIII · 2

THE MOON

O · 3

THE FOOL

IXX · 1

THE SUN

HOW DO I FIND LOVE?

One of the most common questions asked in tarot readings is: How do I find love? When? Where? We may still be wounded by a past relationship that went wrong. We may have been single for a long time and feel we "ought" to be in a relationship like everyone else. We may sabotage our chances of finding new love, because we unconsciously project energies that put potential lovers off, or we simply attract the "wrong" people to us. But the tarot can point us in the right direction, or at least help us to understand our current problem.

This spread will help you challenge your own belief in what the "right" person is for you. It will also enable you to look a little into the future (your own projection, remember) to see who or what is about to come into your life and, more importantly, how to go about making it happen.

LAYING THE CARDS
This spread resembles the bricks of a wall to symbolize the usually unconscious building blocks of your character, which are revealed at the moment you lay down the cards.

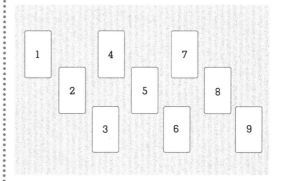

1. You now
2. What's stopping you from finding love?
3. The kind of lover you need
4. What you must express
5. What you must give
6. What you must take
7. How you will find love
8. The kind of love who will come into your life
9. The outcome

In this example reading, I have included possible "reactions" to the reading to show how, sometimes, the tarot doesn't give us the answers we want to hear!

EXAMPLE READING

1. **Seven of Swords:** I currently escape responsibilities in some way.
2. **Eight of Wands:** I'm all over the place, and I just don't seem to meet anyone who can keep up with me.
3. **The Magician:** The kind of lover I need is an achiever. (But I avoid these types of people…am I missing something here?)
4. **Eight of Pentacles:** I need to express that I want to achieve more. (Maybe I am being honest at last?)
5. **Two of Pentacles:** I must give out my fun-loving spirit.
6. **Three of Swords:** I must accept that others have been hurt too.
7. **The Hierophant:** I will find love through further education, courses, or classes in something I am passionate about.
8. **King of Swords:** The kind of lover who will come into my life is intellectually knowledgeable, strong, and assertive.
9. **Two of Swords:** I may resist, put up barriers, and blind myself to the truth. (I am in denial in some way. I mustn't cut myself off from someone who may be the ideal partner.)

LOVE TEST

If you're single, you can use this spread to help you find new romance. It is also useful for helping to make a relationship work, and how to move forward in that partnership. This spread simply tests your integrity about what you really want, and if you're really being honest with yourself.

LAYING THE CARDS

As you lay out the cards, think about what love truly means to you. Is love about total commitment or marriage, or are you a secret romantic who wants to have the freedom to roam?

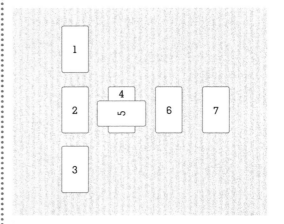

1. My love objective
2. What I can offer
3. What I lack
4. What I look for in a relationship
5. What influences are blocking me
6. The heart of the matter
7. How can I make this work?

EXAMPLE READING

This example explores how you can make a relationship work and includes what you might hear yourself saying upon asking the questions.

1. **Five of Cups:** My objective is to have the kind of love I once had and lost. (Regrets indeed!)
2. **Page of Wands:** I can offer an adventurous spirit. (Could that attract someone?)
3. **Seven of Pentacles:** I lack focus. (Really? No, I don't believe it. Well maybe…)
4. **The Tower:** I want chaos and uncertainty; I like living on the edge. (Maybe that's true…)

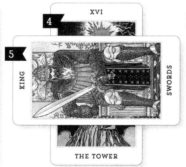

5. **King of Swords:** My rigid thinking and resistance to change is blocking progress.
6. **The Hanged Man:** I must accept that life can be viewed from other angles.
7. **Six of Pentacles:** I can make this relationship work by giving and taking. (Balance and harmony are missing, that's true.)

MIRRORING

This is a great spread for discovering what someone else is thinking or feeling about you, at any one moment. Remember, if you are totally honest, it will help you to respect your partner or your date's perspective of you and the relationship. Do make sure you are objective about your partner's answers!

LAYING THE CARDS

Lay out the cards as shown. Read the cards either one at a time, or you can read your cards first, followed by your partner's.

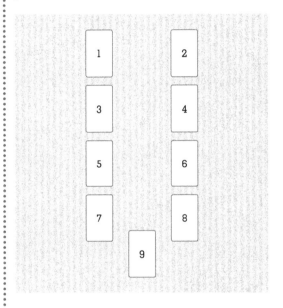

1. Who I am right now
2. Who you are right now
3. This is what I feel now
4. This is what you feel now
5. This is what I want from the relationship
6. This is what you want from the relationship
7. This is how I see the relationship going
8. This is how you see the relationship going
9. This is the outcome

1. CUPS — IV

2. THE WHEEL — X

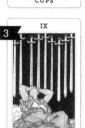

3. SWORDS — IX

4. PENTACLES — X

5. WANDS — KING

6. CUPS — VII

7. SWORDS — X

8. THE SUN — XXI

9. WANDS — V

In this example, extremes of energy are used for the two people in this relationship. The "I" or A partner is fraught by doubt, the "you" or B partner is carefree and up for romance. Sometimes, it helps to even "set up" an example for yourself of an imaginary couple before reading your own personal mirrored relationship.

1. **Four of Cups:** I am rather withdrawn and introspective; I am not sure what is on offer.
2. **The Wheel of Fortune:** You are living for the moment, fairly carefree about life.
3. **Nine of Swords:** I feel guilty, worried, and vulnerable, unsure of everything.
4. **Ten of Pentacles:** You feel happy enjoying the good life, and you are at one with the world.
5. **King of Wands:** I want this relationship to be dramatic and powerful.
6. **Seven of Cups:** You want the relationship to be self-indulgent, fanciful.
7. **Ten of Swords:** I see it all ending in disaster.
8. **The Sun:** You see it merely as a game.
9. **Five of Wands:** The outcome is that we will always be at odds with each other, unless we try to find mutual desires and goals.

Conclusion—we need to look at how we can compromise our very different views of life and love.

"OUCH!"

The last of the relationship spreads is about hurt feelings. This tells you about what can cause the wounds between the people in a relationship. By working with this insight, you can see the relationship with more honesty and clarity. You will discover how to overcome those things that set off our defense mechanisms, and spark disagreements and moods.

LAYING THE CARDS

This spread is slightly different because we're going to use only the suits Cups and Swords for choosing the first six cards. They must be separated from the deck and shuffled together. After choosing the six cards, remove and shuffle the Major Arcana separately, and choose one card to give you the final position.

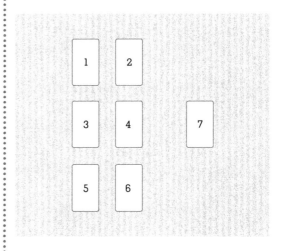

1. How I love you
2. How I hurt you
3. How I defend myself
4. How you love me
5. How you hurt me
6. How you defend yourself
7. What we can do about it

EXAMPLE READING

1. **Knight of Swords:** I love you in a very frank, direct, and sometimes demanding way.
2. **Two of Swords:** I hurt you because I don't give away my feelings, and I put up emotional barriers.
3. **Seven of Cups:** I defend myself by believing everything will be all right if I don't say anything.
4. **Nine of Swords:** You love me in an anxious, guilty way.

5. **Ace of Swords:** You hurt me by being telling me I'm wrong and you're right all the time.
6. **Three of Cups:** You defend yourself by saying everyone's your friend and you don't need only one person.
7. **Judgment:** Moving forward, we can drop old values and try to see there is no one to blame, certainly not each other.

MYSTIC SEVEN

This spread uses the mystical number seven and offers you the key to the archetypal energy that will be operating in your favor in the weeks to come. If you develop the specific quality associated with the numerological energy, you will achieve fantastic results.

ARCHETYPAL ENERGIES

Add the number of the outcome card (in this example Temperance is fourteen) to seven, and then add again to bring to one digit. So, for example, $14 + 7 = 21$, $2+1 = 3$.

Now look in the box below to see the archetypal energy for this spread. This is the energy you must express. In the example above, to truly make sure you "achieve your dream," you would be a Communicator, and all forms of communication are favored if you initiate that quality.

1. The Innovator
2. The Negotiator
3. The Communicator
4. The Organizer
5. The Traveler
6. The Healer
7. The Artist/Philosopher
8. The Entrepreneur
9. The Crusader

LAYING THE CARDS

Don't try to interpret the cards as you lay them out, just let yourself go with the flow of the spread. When you place the final card down you may even have a flash of insight into what it will mean when its number is added to 7.

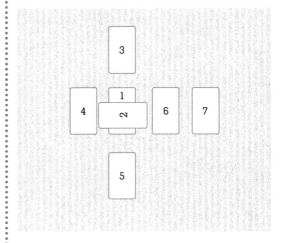

1. You now
2. The blockage
3. Your expectations
4. Recent influences
5. Forthcoming positive influences
6. What to avoid in the future
7. The outcome—card's number, plus seven

As usual, shuffle the cards and place them face up in the order shown.

EXAMPLE READING

1. **Justice:** You are currently feeling that life is about compromise, but that's fair isn't it?
2. **The Chariot:** Someone controlling is taking advantage of your good nature.
3. **Ace of Cups:** You want life to be a beautiful, exciting thing—not boring.
4. **Ten of Swords:** Recently, you've felt that life and people have been against you.
5. **The Wheel of Fortune:** You will soon have a chance to take a leap of faith and get out of this monotony.
6. **Two of Wands:** Avoid being too idealistic. Dream, yes, but dream realistically.
7. **Temperance:** Modify your plans, take your time to see what dream you can really achieve.

CUPS

SWORDS

JUSTICE

WANDS

TEMPERANCE

THE WHEEL

CELTIC CROSS

Now that you have worked your way through basic to more complicated spreads, you've learned two important things:

First, there's no point interpreting each card individually without referring or relating it to the question.

Second, the focus card is usually symbolized by the first card—it's the protagonist or the star of the show. All the other cards are merely other characters on the stage who add depth and resonance to the story. (There will be tarot readers who disagree with this, but personally, as a beginner, you need a direction to follow. Later, when you are more advanced, you can decide exactly how you interpret spreads. This is a method that works and will enable you to get to know all the cards as you go along.)

Destiny spreads are those we often turn to when we need to delve ahead and see where we might be next week, or in a few months' time. These are the most traditional kind of tarot reading.

LAYING THE CARDS

This traditional spread gives you a range of future options and influences to think about regarding any specific issue. Personally, I would use this if you want some objective direction for your life journey for no more than a month or so ahead. Before you shuffle and choose the cards, do think about a general problem that needs to be resolved. Lay the cards face up in the order as shown.

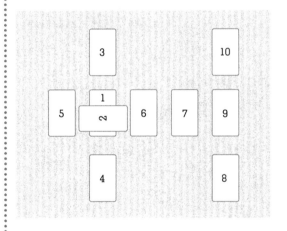

1. You now/Heart of the matter
2. Blockage/challenge
3. Conscious goal
4. Unknown influence
5. Recent negative influence
6. Approaching short-term influence
7. Forthcoming resources
8. How others will perceive you
9. Long-term influence
10. Long-term outcome

EXAMPLE READING

Question: I'm desperate to change my career, will I have the right opportunities?

1. **Five of Wands:** I'm feeling quite competitive and ready to rise to a challenge.
2. **Knight of Cups:** I'm being too idealistic about the opportunities that could arise.
3. **The Magician:** My conscious goal is to manifest my creative ideas.
4. **The Empress:** A creative female will, unknown to me, help me to move ahead.
5. **The Devil:** A materialistic colleague has put me down, so I didn't believe I was capable of change.
6. **Three of Pentacles:** A group or team of people will be important for my future.
7. **The Star:** New inspiration and sudden insights will come to me.
8. **The Chariot:** Others will see me as motivated and dynamic.
9. **King of Wands:** A reliable, powerful male will be a long-term influence on my success.
10. **The High Priestess:** I will be in charge of my life; my creativity will flow in the right career for me.

THE MAGICIAN

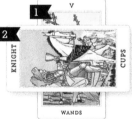

THE DEVIL

KNIGHT

CUPS

WANDS

PENTACLES

THE STAR

WANDS

THE HIGH PRIESTESS

THE EMPRESS

THE CHARIOT

THE GYPSY SPREAD

Another traditional spread, the gypsy spread threads together the past, present, and future with seven areas of your life. You can either read this spread line by line, or in columns, as themes: work—past, present, and future; home—past, present, and future, and so on.

As there is not enough space here for an example reading of the whole spread, here are three theme examples corresponding to the numbers in the diagram for Love, Goals, and Life Journey.

LAYING THE CARDS
Lay the cards out in the order shown. You can either choose individual cards from the pack or after shuffling, just cut the deck once and take one card after another from the top of the deck.

LINE A the past
LINE B the present
LINE C the future

I. Work
II. Home
III. Luck
IV. Friends
V. Love
VI. Goals
VII. Life Journey

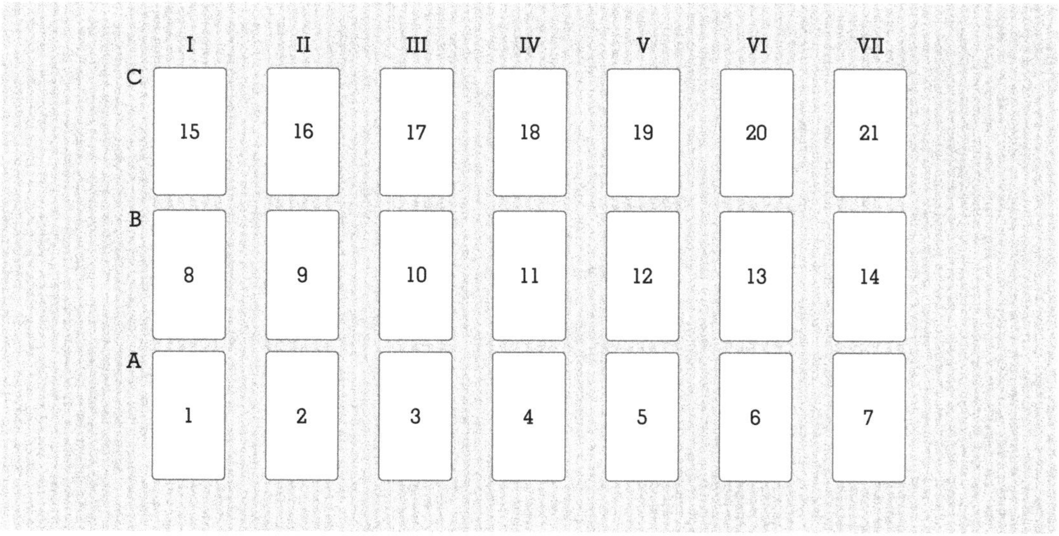

	I	II	III	IV	V	VI	VII
C	15	16	17	18	19	20	21
B	8	9	10	11	12	13	14
A	1	2	3	4	5	6	7

LOVE

19. **The Tower:** In the future, I'm going to get out of my rut and change my life for the better.

12. **The Four of Pentacles:** Right now, I'm clinging to the known because it feels safer.

5. **The Fool:** In the past, I was so infatuated I didn't stop to see what was really going on.

GOALS

20. **The Hanged Man:** In the future, I will be able to see my goals from a new perspective and realize what needs to change.

13. **Seven of Pentacles:** Right now, I need to evaluate my life and see what I want for the future

6. **Ten of Cups:** In the past, I felt content just

LIFE JOURNEY

21. **The World:** In the future, I'm going to widen my horizons and go where I want to go, whatever others think or say.

14. **Five of Wands:** Right now, there's so much hostility and loved ones just don't understand me.

7. **Two of Wands:** I used to want to explore the world.

THE YEAR AHEAD

We all want to know about the future, it seems. Often we'd like to know how our lives will progress over the course of a year. Fixed as we are by the constraints of human-made time, the "year" seems to us to encapsulate all our missions and goals in its twelve-month cycle. This spread will help you understand the opportunities available to you each month. It is based on the astrological year, starting in April. But start reading with the card that represents the month ahead. For example, if it were August when you did the reading, you'd start from the sixth card, giving you the energy for September.

LAYING THE CARDS

For this spread, shuffle as usual, then cut the deck three times. From each of the three decks take the first four cards rather than choosing randomly. In other words, from deck one, place the first four cards at positions 1–4, from the second deck place the first four cards at positions 5–8, and from the last deck, positions 9–12.

1. April
2. May
3. June
4. July
5. August
6. September
7. October
8. November
9. December
10. January
11. February
12. March

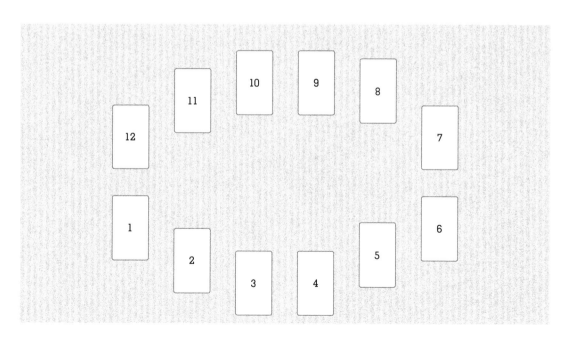

EXAMPLE READING:

As there is not enough room to summarize a complete spread, here are the first months of the year, according to someone who did the reading in August, as above.

6. **September—Four of Pentacles:** There will be financial opportunities for you to profit from or invest in. Don't try to be too controlling or possessive.

7. **October—The Hermit:** You need to reflect on life, take a break from the rat race and see what has made you feel happiest in the past, then you can act on that information.

8. **November—The Lovers:** Choices need to be made; you will be on a crusade for passion or need to attend to your close relationships.

9. **December—Ten of Pentacles:** Plans are beginning to work out, and you will have a run of good fortune. Keep at it—your mission is just beginning.

10. **January—Three of Cups:** Great opportunities arise where you can put your trust in others and share your creative thoughts.

11. **February—Three of Swords:** You'll be able to get to the heart of an emotional matter.

12. **March—Six of Swords:** You will be able to move away from emotionally troubled waters or leave the past behind.

THE LABYRINTH

The last spread is a little more complicated and is designed to stretch your own powers of interpretation.

The labyrinth is an ancient symbol for self-discovery. This spread, inspired by the labyrinth, enables you to explore four pathways. These are associated with the four elements, the four cardinal directions, and the four suits of the tarot.

The paths are:
The path to the north: The path of prosperity, associated with Earth and Pentacles.
The path to the east: The path of wisdom, associated with Air and Swords.
The path to the south: The path of passion, associated with Fire and Wands.
The path to the west: The path of feelings, associated with Water and Cups.

LAYING THE CARDS

Lay the cards out as in the diagram, facedown. Then, choose a path according to your first choice.

These paths are all important to you, but after interpreting all four paths separately, you'll know which one to follow and attend to right now, even if it isn't the first path you chose. With each pathway, ask yourself the following questions corresponding to each of the four cards:

1. What does this direction mean for me?
2. What gift will I receive from following this path?
3. What challenges will I face?
4. What is the outcome if I follow this path?

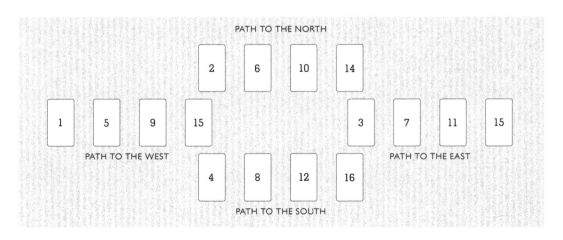

PATH TO THE NORTH

2 6 10 14

1 5 9 15 3 7 11 15

PATH TO THE WEST

PATH TO THE EAST

4 8 12 16

PATH TO THE SOUTH

EXAMPLE READING

Example reading from the path of prosperity, the north:

1   VI

THE LOVERS

2   I

WANDS

3   X

WANDS

4   KNIGHT

PENTACLES

1. **The Lovers:** If I follow the path of prosperity, I must make conscious choices and be true to my values.
2. **Ace of Wands:** If I follow this path, I will receive the gift of great opportunities.
3. **Ten of Wands:** The challenges I will face are taking on too much at once, or becoming a slave to my desires, which I might later regret or resent.
4. **Knight of Pentacles:** The outcome, if I follow this path, is to show I can be persistent and dedicated. I can be organized and realistic, but I need to embrace potentials and not fear adapting to situations as they arise.

Once you have completed the four pathways, you will know which one is the right one to follow. If you are able to take on all pathways, then the challenge is there for you to show that you are at one with the universal energies, embracing all that is a reflection of yourself.

MAJOR ARCANA SPELL

Throughout this book, you've learned how to read, interpret, and understand the meaning of the mirrored images you see before you. In a deeper sense, that means you are learning about you.

For your last exercise, and to take an entirely new angle on the tarot, we're going to look at another way of using the cards—for spells and enchantments.

This is a fun way of getting to know the colors, moods, and energies behind the Major Arcana, and it can lead you onto other ways of using the tarot, expanding your repertoire and understanding as you go.

1. From the chart on the next page, choose a colored candle and a card for the spell you want to perform.

2. In front of a mirror, sit down and light the candle; and place the next corresponding tarot card to the candle, face up.

3. Relax and close your eyes for a few minutes to invoke the power of the Universe. Touch the tarot card and concentrate on the image. Open your eyes and gaze at the candle flame reflected in the mirror, and repeat the name of the tarot card three times. Follow it with a spell of your choice, for example:

> *"Justice, Justice, Justice—bring me the power of…negotiation."*

4. Close your eyes again, still touching the tarot card. Concentrate on the card's image in your mind, and then open your eyes. Blow out the candle and the spell is cast.

XIV

TEMPERANCE

CARDS	CANDLE COLORS	SPELLS
The Fool	White	For new beginnings, children, creativity
The Magician	Yellow	For banishing deception
The High Priestess	Lavender	For feminine power, spiritual growth
The Empress	Pink	For marriage, fertility, loyalty
The Emperor	Dark Blue	For success, career issues, empowerment
The Hierophant	Purple	For wisdom, finding lost objects
The Lovers	Green	For love spells, romance, harmony
The Chariot	Crimson	For favorable travel, progress
Strength	Wine red	For beneficial control and self-confidence
The Hermit	Ivory	For letting go of the past
The Wheel of Fortune	Orange	For money matters and good fortune
Justice	Grey	For decision-making, good negotiation
The Hanged Man	Dark Green	For giving up addictions
Death	Black	For accepting change
Temperance	Lilac	For cooling ardor or calming others
The Devil	Ochre	For overcoming fear or self-doubt
The Tower	Vanilla	For property issues, protection
The Star	Pale yellow	For fame, recognition, success
The Moon	Silver	For beauty, peace, attracting others
The Sun	Gold or bright yellow	For happy days, creativity
Judgment	Indigo	For forgiveness, breaking free
The World	Violet	For new ventures, travel, and fulfillment

CONCLUSION

We have come to the end of these key exercises, and like the Fool we have come full circle, but the journey has not yet ended. In fact, the tarot journey is never-ending. As you learn more and more about the tarot, you become aware of yourself as part of the Universe, not separate from it.

Once you are a little more familiar with the tarot, you can combine it with other techniques such as using crystals, numerology, the Kabbalah, and so much more. These ancient arts are all part of the same tapestry of the Universe, connecting everything as One.

You can start to develop and create your own tarot spreads by working with ideas, numbers, themes, and so on. The main thing to remember is to keep the spreads simple so that they can be easily interpreted. Make a note of spread designs in your journal. Use your inner self as your guide.

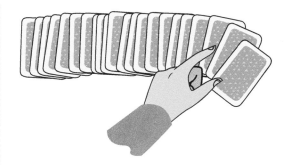

READING FOR OTHERS

Practicing on your friends and family is a good way to get to know the cards too. However, we all tend to project our ideas and feelings onto the qualities represented by the cards. You might think the Death card is transformative, while someone else might loathe the image or not want to change.

When you start reading for others, make it a fun experience. Try to be as objective as possible; be aware that the more you know someone and their life history, the more subjective you'll be.

Reading the tarot for strangers is the most surprising and revealing way to learn the tarot, simply because you have no hidden agendas. Before you embark

on reading for strangers, do remember the tarot golden rule: the tarot does not lie, only people do.

Remember how the vicar's wife told me I would meet a blonde man who would be with me forever? Once I got back from my Paris romantic adventure, I worked in the music business, and on my many travels across Europe, I met a blonde man who I fell in love with. Sadly, it all ended badly, with a fair dose of betrayal thrown in. The vicar's wife had indeed identified two influences in my life, but she had decided in her own mind what was better for me and got it wrong. Although I never saw the dark stranger again, we parted friends, and he has stayed in my heart, forever a part of me. This is a lesson to be learned when reading for others—don't make judgments, don't project your desires or fantasies onto others, and most importantly, don't do so to yourself.

The tarot is a journey indeed, and like many journeys, it's often the path we hadn't intended to go down, which leads us to somewhere life-changing and awakening.

Remember the Fool's bag you unpacked as the last exercise in the Major Arcana chapter? It is time to take your list out of the box and look at it. Does it hold the same meaning for you as before?

If not, maybe it's time to make a new list as you prepare for the next stage of your tarot journey.

Enjoy, and let the light of the Universe shine through you every day.

GLOSSARY

ARCHETYPE
A universal energy or pattern of behavior which operates autonomously in the depths of the human psyche.

ASTROLOGY
An ancient system of divination which studies the patterns and placement of the planets of the solar system as they appear to travel through the zodiac belt.

BLOCKAGE CARD
This is a tarot card that crosses or sits at right angles on top of another card when placed within a spread.

CELTIC CROSS
One of the most popular—and believed to be the oldest—tarot spreads known in mystical circles. The spread, based on the symbol of a Celtic cross found throughout Ireland, is laid out with the vertical columns representing our spiritual quest and the horizontal line of cards representing the individual's journey.

CHAKRA
Many Eastern traditions maintain that a system of subtle energy flows through the body, linked by seven or more energy centers known as chakras.

DIVINATION
Originates in the Latin word "*divines*," meaning "to be inspired by the gods," and now means "to foresee, foretell, or predict."

ELEMENTS
The four "elements," Fire, Earth, Air, and Water, are used in astrology and represent qualities and energies characteristic in four types of individual.

FOCUS CARD
A card which is often the first card drawn in a spread, but it can also be a card which is particularly significant or "speaks" to the querent.

FUTURE OUTCOME CARD
A card that is placed in the last position of a spread usually signifies the outcome of the issue involved. It is also a stepping stone to the next stage of your journey.

KABBALAH
An ancient Hebrew esoteric pathway which offers profound insight and spiritual wisdom. Derived from the Hebrew word meaning "to receive." The core element to the Kabbalah is the symbol of the tree of life, a blueprint for the Universe which attempts to reveal the interconnectedness of all aspects of life.

MAJOR ARCANA
The 22 cards of the tarot deck which convey powerful archetypal images and are symbolic of both the deeper aspects of our being and of universal themes and experiences.

MINOR ARCANA
Made up of four suits of 14 cards, these 56 cards represent day-to-day aspects of our lives.

NUMEROLOGY
The art of divining using numbers, which are considered pivotal to the workings of the Universe. The primary numbers 1 to 9 each vibrate to a different frequency, and these vibrations occur throughout the Universe. This was thought to be an expression of the stars and planets, which themselves had their own numerical value and harmonic.

OCCULT
From the Latin "occults," meaning hidden or mysterious. It was used from the fifteenth century as a verb meaning "to conceal," but was later used in the nineteenth century to describe supernatural or magical beliefs and practices.

OPEN READING
A reading where no questions are asked and the cards are read without relating them to any specific issue.

ORDER OF THE GOLDEN DAWN
An influential occultist group founded by doctor and freemason William Wynn Westcott and flamboyant society gentleman Samuel Mathers in 1888. Mathers fused Egyptian esoteric systems with medieval magical texts and Eastern spiritual beliefs to create a workable magic system.

PENTACLE
A magical object or talisman, usually disc-shaped, and used as a symbol for the element Earth. As a suit in the tarot it is also referred to as a disc, or coin. The word derives from the Latin "pentaculum," related to the pentagram or five-pointed mystical star.

PIPS
Small shapes or symbols shown on the numbered cards of tarot decks (and also on normal playing cards) to define the nature and number of the suit. The Five of Wands will show five wands and the number five. However, most modern tarot suits have a pictorial image to reveal the "message" behind the number shown.

PROJECTION
An unconscious process whereby we see in a person, thing, object, event, or experience the potentials, flaws, hates, and loves that actually belong to ourselves.

REVERSED CARDS

Cards laid down in a spread whose imagery appears upside down from the reader's perspective when turned face up.

SPREAD

A lay-out of cards which form a specific pattern, often of great symbolic power in itself and of mystical significance.

SYMBOL

Something that represents something else by association, including abstract shapes, material objects, and mystical patterns which often represent something numinous or occult.

SYNCHRONICITY

Psychologist Carl Jung coined this term to describe "meaningful coincidences": coincidences that are meaningful to the person who experiences them. He believed that the choice of tarot card we select is prompted by something deep within that needs to be expressed or become manifest in the world at that moment in time.

THOTH

An Egyptian god, equivalent to the Greek god, Hermes, Thoth was believed to be the inventor of hieroglyphics and mystical letters or symbols which occult scholars recognized in the tarot.

UNIVERSAL WELL OF KNOWLEDGE

The universal well of knowledge is where all thoughts, ideas, beliefs, archetypes, memories, and behavior is to be found, deep within ourselves at the core of the Universe.

"YOU NOW" CARD

The first card you lay down in a spread reveals the current state of you, the querent, and issues that need to be addressed right now.

FURTHER READING

Bartlett, Sarah.
The Tarot Bible.
New York, US: Sterling, 2006.

Pollack, Rachel.
78 Degrees of Wisdom.
Newburyport, US: Weiser Books, 2007.

Bunning, Joan.
Learning the Tarot.
Newburyport, US: Weiser Books, 1998.

Sharman Burke, Juliet, and Liz Greene.
The New Mythic Tarot.
New York, US: St Martin's Press, 2011.

Greer, Mary K.
Tarot for Yourself.
Wayne, US: New Page Books, 2002.

Dean, Liz.
The Ultimate Guide to Tarot.
Beverly, US: Fair Winds Press, 2015

USEFUL WEBSITES

Astrodienst
www.astro.com

American Tarot Association
www.ata-tarot.com

Learning the Tarot
www.learntarot.com

Tarot Association of the British Isles
www.tabi.org.uk

Tarosophy Tarot Association
www.tarotassociation.net

The Astrology Room
www.theastrologyroom.com

INDEX

KNIGHT

PENTACLES

VI

THE LOVERS

CREDITS

Tarot cards reproduced with the kind permission of Lo Scarabeo s.r.l. www.loscarabeo.com
Universal Tarot © Lo Scarabeo s.r.l. All rights reserved.

p8 © Chronicle | Alamy
p9 © Tony Moran | Shutterstock
p12 left © Classic Image | Alamy
right © V&A Images | Alamy
p13 © : BasPhoto | Shutterstock
p14 © John McKenna | Alamy
p15 © Martin McCarthy | iStock
p16 © Photos 12 | Alamy
p18 © Fribus Mara | Shutterstock

p23 © Balazs Kovacs Images | Shutterstock
p24 © aleksandr hunta | Shutterstock
p29 © Ammentorp Photography | Shutterstock
p30 © Studio_3321 | Shutterstock
p32 © Photology1971 | Shutterstock
p57 © nikkytok | Shutterstock
p63 © Nikki Zalewski | Shutterstock
p73 © VICUSCHKA | Shutterstock
p83 © J. Palys | Shutterstock
© olegganko| Shutterstock
© Skylines | Shutterstock
p85 © kearia | Shutterstock
p131 © gmnicholas | iStock